GLOBAL
CITIZENSHIP
ENGAGE IN THE POLITICS OF A
CHANGING WORLD

JULIE KNUTSON
Illustrated by Traci Van Wagoner

Nomad Press

A division of Nomad Communications

10 9 8 7 6 5 4 3 2 1

Copyright © 2020 by Nomad Press. All rights reserved.

No part of this book may be reproduced in any form without permission in writing from the publisher, except by a reviewer who may quote brief passages in a
review or **for limited educational use**. The trademark "Nomad Press" and the Nomad Press logo are trademarks of Nomad Communications, Inc.

This book was manufactured by Versa Press, Inc.
September 2020, Job #J20-04491
ISBN Softcover: 978-1-61930-936-4
ISBN Hardcover: 978-1-61930-933-3

Educational Consultant, Marla Conn

Questions regarding the ordering of this book should be addressed to
Nomad Press
2456 Christian St., White River Junction, VT 05001
www.nomadpress.net
Printed in the United States.

More Social Studies titles in the Inquire & Investigate series

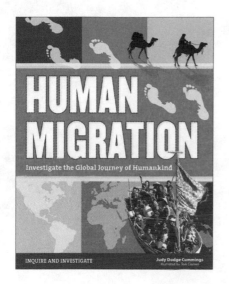

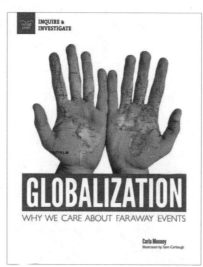

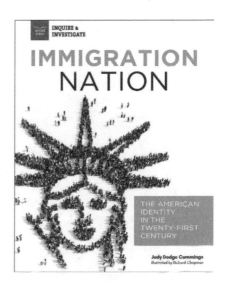

Check out more titles at www.nomadpress.net

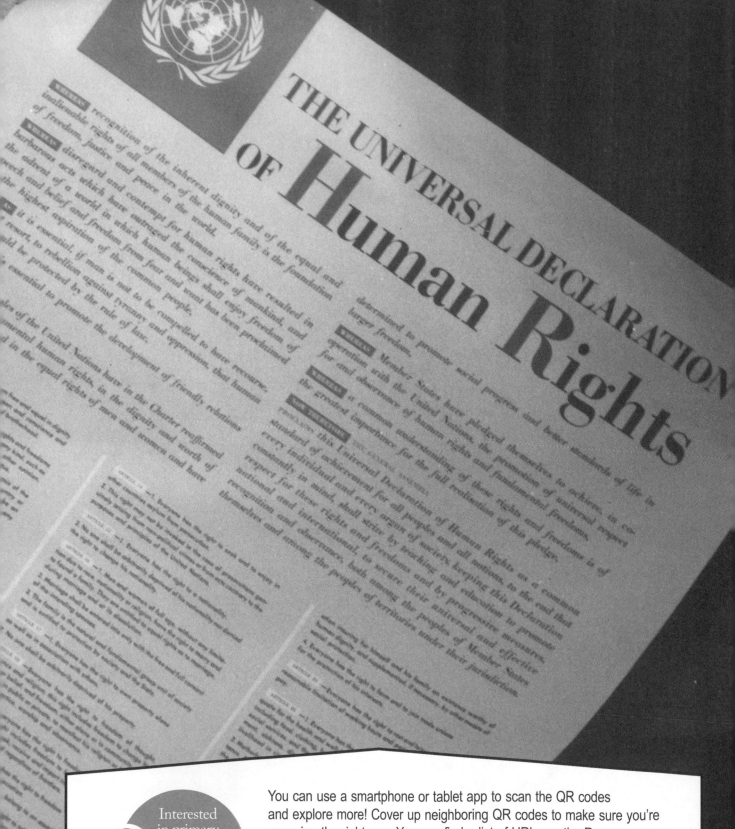

THE UNIVERSAL DECLARATION
OF Human Rights

Interested in primary sources?

Look for this icon.

You can use a smartphone or tablet app to scan the QR codes and explore more! Cover up neighboring QR codes to make sure you're scanning the right one. You can find a list of URLs on the Resources page.

If the QR code doesn't work, try searching the internet with the Keyword Prompts to find other helpful sources.

 global citizenship

Contents

TIMELINE

539 BCE: Cyrus the Great conquers Babylon. The so-called *Cyrus Cylinder*—often considered the first human rights document—informs Babylonians of their rights.

circa 500 BCE: Confucius advances the "Golden Rule"—"Do not do unto others what you do not want done to yourself"—in China.

circa 1200 CE: The Mandingo Empire in West Africa establishes the *Manden Charter*, an orally transmitted constitution. The charter provides for a number of rights—education, food security, freedom of expression, and the abolition of slavery by raid.

1215 CE: Aristocrats in England force King John to sign the *Magna Carta*. This document limits the king's power and guarantees certain rights to royal subjects.

Eighteenth century: Enlightenment ideas spread. These are based on the belief that humans possess reason and can create better societies.

Eighteenth and nineteenth centuries: Abolitionists work within and across national boundaries to end the Atlantic slave trade.

1864: The First Geneva Convention sets international law to protect victims of war and establishes the Red Cross as an aid organization. The Geneva Convention is revised in 1906, 1929, and 1949.

1899 and 1907: International delegates come together in the Netherlands for the Hague Conventions. Global standards are set for the laws of war and handling disarmament and war crimes.

1920: The League of Nations is established as a diplomatic forum to resolve conflicts and avoid war. The organization also assists with early refugee crises, including the rescue of Armenian genocide survivors.

1930: Gandhi leads the Salt March, a nonviolent protest against colonial occupation in India.

1939 to 1945: More than 6 million Jewish people are murdered in the Holocaust. Homosexuals, people with disabilities, and Roma and Polish people are also killed in mass numbers.

1944: The World Bank and International Monetary Fund are established.

1945: The United Nations (UN) is established as an intergovernmental organization to prevent future wars and promote international cooperation.

1948: The UN adopts the Universal Declaration of Human Rights, which lists fundamental human rights.

1948–1960: African and Asian countries decolonize, asserting their rights to independence from European rule.

1960s–1970s: Civil rights movements worldwide uphold that all people should be guaranteed rights, regardless of race, gender, or sexual orientation.

1986: The African Commission on Human and People's Rights takes effect after seven years of development.

1989: The UN Convention on the Rights of the Child is adopted.

1993: The European Union is established, increasing trade and travel between European states.

2000: The UN releases the Millennium Development Goals.

2015: The UN adopts the Paris Agreement to address climate change.

2015: The UN releases the Sustainable Development Goals, which are 17 global priorities to be met by 2030.

2019: Global youth activism around climate change surges, with #FridaysfortheFuture and the Youth Climate Strike movement.

2020: The UN releases results from its first Gender Social Norms Index, which show that nearly 90 percent of people worldwide hold biases against women.

March 2020: The World Health Organization declares the coronavirus, or COVID-19, outbreak a pandemic.

May 25, 2020: George Floyd, a 46-year-old African American man, dies at the hands of Minneapolis, Minnesota, police. Video footage shows a white officer pinning a handcuffed Floyd to the ground with a knee on his neck for almost nine minutes while Floyd repeatedly cries out, "I can't breathe." Outrage and waves of protest calling out racial profiling, bias, and violence in policing ensue in cities worldwide.

Introduction ▶

What Makes a Citizen?

HOW MANY OF YOU KNOW THE PARABLE OF THE HUMMINGBIRD?

What makes a citizen "global?"

Global citizens think of themselves as residents of the whole world. This is an identity that is both free of and complementary to the borders and boundaries that frame other kinds of identity, such as national and local.

• • • • • • • • •

There is a parable common to many cultures that begins with a burning forest. Some of the woodland creatures that call this forest home are trapped, while others flee at the first whiff of smoke. Most of the animals watch—stunned, afraid, and powerless—as fire destroys their habitat. But then one, tiny hummingbird makes a decision.

Instead of standing on the sidelines, this little bird flies to the nearest stream, collects droplets of water on its wings, and flies back to try to extinguish the fire. Back and forth it goes, despite the flames that singe its feathers and the teasing of the other animals. As small as it is, this hummingbird refuses to stand by as its home burns and vows to do the best it can to put out the fire.

Parables are meant to teach a lesson, and there's one to be learned here. When faced with a challenge, we have a choice: We can be like the hummingbird—actively tackling the problems before us—or we can stand by and watch.

This book is designed to show you how you can take action to become more like this courageous little bird. What problems in your community, and in the broader world, do you want to solve? What steps can you take to address them? And how do you find friends and allies to fly with as you take on these tasks?

ARE YOU A GLOBAL CITIZEN?

Our hummingbird in the story exhibits two key qualities of citizenship—awareness and responsibility. The bird is aware of what's happening in the forest and sees the effect this dangerous situation will have on the community. Armed with this knowledge, the hummingbird assumes responsibility to protect its environment.

The bird is also action-oriented—it takes creative steps to confront the challenge. Plus, the bird isn't easily discouraged. In some versions of the story, this persistent creature convinces others to follow its lead.

Just like the hummingbird, global citizens are conscious of what's happening in their world. They educate themselves on issues that impact all of the communities to which they belong—local, national, and global. Global citizens know their rights as human beings and recognize that certain rights are guaranteed to all people on the planet.

Global citizens also recognize that with rights come responsibilities. They understand that big, planetary problems such as climate change and pandemics, including the COVID-19 outbreak of 2020, are borderless. People need to work together across boundaries to solve them. They seek opportunities to educate peers, defend rights, and take actions to create a more just world.

In 2004, Wangari Maathai (1940–) received the Nobel Peace Prize. Maathai is best-known for launching Kenya's Green Belt Movement, which sought to address environmental problems such as habitat loss, food shortages, and soil erosion, all resulting from deforestation. She and her allies tackled this problem by replanting millions of trees across the country. In the process, they created new opportunities for education, environmental awareness, gender equality, and democratic engagement in Kenya. You can watch her talk about what the parable of the hummingbird means to her in terms of citizenship and informed action in this video.

Maathai hummingbird

PRIMARY SOURCES

PS

Primary sources come from people who were eyewitnesses to events. They might write about the event, take pictures, post short messages to social media or blogs, or record the event for radio or video. The photographs in this book are primary sources, taken at the time of the event. Paintings of events are usually not primary sources, since they were often painted long after the event took place.

What other primary sources can you find? Why are primary sources important? Do you learn differently from primary sources than from secondary sources, which come from people who did not directly experience the event?

WHAT DOES GLOBAL CITIZENSHIP LOOK LIKE?

Remember the hummingbird from our opening parable? Kids worldwide are following its lead. Activists with the Youth Climate Strike, including Sweden's Greta Thunberg (2003–), are stepping up for the well-being of our planet by using social media and direct action to urge politicians to address climate issues. On March 15 and September 20, 2019, youth worldwide abandoned their daily routines to strike, with the goal of drawing attention to the climate crisis and pushing for a greener future.

In Nashville, Tennessee, in June 2020, a group of six teenaged girls also acted as metaphorical hummingbirds. In mere days, the team of 14- to 16-year-olds organized as Teens4Equality and coordinated a "Black Lives Matter" protest in response to the murder of George Floyd.

Across the world, individuals and groups are pledging to uphold the SDGs.

On June 4, more than 10,000 participants took to Nashville's streets to insist that the human rights of all people are upheld and respected. A teacher of two of the young women noted, "Young people are ready to lead, and we need to step out of the way and let them."

Youth Climate Strikers, Black Lives Matter activists, and countless other young people worldwide are acting on the UN's Sustainable Development Goals (SDGs), a plan for improving our world by 2030. The 17 SDGs were set by the UN General Assembly in 2015 and highlight both what we need to do to create a better planet by 2030 and how we can achieve it as a world community.

> Children and adults across the globe are devising creative, innovative ways to meet these goals.

Today, as the COVID-19 pandemic threatens to roll back progress made in areas such as poverty reduction and gender equality, this creativity and innovation are more important than ever.

CAN I BE A CITIZEN OF MY COUNTRY *AND* THE GLOBE?

When people describe our world as "global," they're talking about the connections and interdependence that exist between citizens in all corners of the world. The roots of globalization are long—people have traveled and traded between continents for thousands of years. What's different today? Pace, reach, and intensity. Developments in travel, communications, and banking allow people, things, and ideas to travel the world both physically and via the internet at a greater speed than ever before.

TRUTH TOLD

The SDGs build on the Millennium Development Goals (MDGs). Between 2000 and 2015, the eight MDGs moved the bar on global progress in poverty reduction, health, education, and gender equity.

BREXIT

Global institutions aren't without critics. In June 2016, voters in Great Britain narrowly approved "Brexit," Britain's plan to leave the European Union (EU). Pro-Brexit voters viewed the EU as an undemocratic impediment to British sovereignty. People wanting to remain pointed to the EU's social and economic benefits, such as the protection of human rights and freedom of movement of people and goods. After several years of negotiations, Britain formally exited the political and economic union on January 31, 2020.

Does the concept of global citizenship seem like a paradox? After all, many people define citizenship by borders and boundaries. Being a citizen—whether of the United States or Uganda, Peru or Pakistan—means holding a birth certificate and passport that bind you to a specific country. This contrasts with something (or someone) global, which is by definition without boundaries.

How can you be a citizen of the world?

We all belong to many identity groups and communities. These memberships are based on different affiliations and loyalties, including family, race, ethnicity, language, social class, sexual orientation, religion, gender, and gender expression. But a sense of belonging in one group doesn't mean that you can't belong to another. Being American or Ugandan or Peruvian or Pakistani doesn't mean that you cannot think and act globally.

Eleanor Roosevelt presents the Universal Declaration of Human Rights in 1948.

Credit: FDR Presidential Library & Museum (CC BY 2.0)

We don't have to put local or national identities in competition with a global identity—they're all a part of who we are and they can all coexist. You can be a citizen of the city of Anchorage, in the state of Alaska, who is also a resident of the United States and Planet Earth. We all have several different identities, a fact of living in the twenty-first century.

This book introduces you to the rights possessed by all people. These rights were spelled out by the UN in its Universal Declaration of Human Rights (UDHR) in 1948. The UDHR was developed after World War II to prevent future wars, genocides, and abuses of power. This document outlines the political, human, economic, environmental, and cultural rights that all people possess from birth to death, regardless of gender, age, ethnicity, ability, or geographic location.

The rights outlined in this book are those with which *all* people are born. We carry them with us throughout our lives. As a global citizen, it's your task to know, protect, and defend them.

Each chapter of *Global Citizenship* focuses on different rights—human, political, economic, environmental, and cultural—that concern global citizens. You'll learn about the changing ideas of rights and citizenship, as well as past and ongoing human rights struggles. We'll also look at economic justice issues, challenges to the health of our planet, and the right to express and experience culture.

KEY QUESTIONS

- **What is global citizenship?**
- **What rights do global citizens protect and defend?**
- **What responsibilities come with global citizenship? How can the UN's SDGs serve as a guide for informed action?**

UNIVERSAL OR LOCAL?

To many people, the norms expressed in the UDHR reflect Western values, meaning that they stem from European and North American traditions. Experts debate whether the best solutions to conflict are universal or local. Many argue that more traditional, culturally rooted approaches to justice are better suited to conflict resolution. What do you think?

TRUTH TOLD

In February 2020, UN Secretary General António Guterres noted that a "pandemic drives home the essential interconnectedness of our human family." He added, "Preventing the further spread of COVID-19 is a shared responsibility for us all." This idea of shared responsibility is the cornerstone of global citizenship.

MY WORLD

Through the My World Survey, people can identify which of the 17 SDGs matter most to them. At the My World website, you can take the survey and select six SDG priority areas. You can also view results by country to see what people care about across the globe.

My World 2030

- **Do some research and think about the SDG that matters most to you.** Use the library, internet, and local media to research what is being done to address this goal in your community. What organizations are working on this issue? What progress has been made?

- **Visit the "My World Survey" results page at this website.** Compare your responses to the global totals. Which of your selections overlap with those of other respondents?

My World results

- **Filter the survey to view results from your country.** How do your national results compare to the global results? Which of your selections overlap with those of other respondents from your country?

To investigate more, encourage other students and teachers in your school to take the My World survey. Collect and tally the results. Which SDGs emerge as most important? How can you and your classmates address them?

Chapter 1 ▶
Protecting All Human Rights

SOME THINK HUMAN RIGHTS BEGAN WITH ELEANOR ROOSEVELT AND THE *UDHR* IN 1948, BUT THEY REALLY BEGAN **2,000** YEARS EARLIER IN BABYLON.

What are human rights?

IN 539 BCE, CYPRUS THE GREAT CONQUERED THE ENSLAVED CITY OF BABYLON AND GAVE THEM THE CYRUS CYLINDER.

THIS CLAY CYLINDER INFORMED EVERYONE OF THEIR RIGHTS AS NEWLY FREED PEOPLE.

Human Rights

IN AN INTERCONNECTED WORLD, HUMAN RIGHTS ARE FUNDAMENTAL. WE AS GLOBAL CITIZENS OWE IT TO ONE ANOTHER TO PROTECT THEM.

Everyone on the planet has specific rights that ideally enable them to live their lives with health and dignity. These rights include freedom from torture and slavery, the right to an education, and freedom of expression.

● ● ● ● ● ● ● ● ●

Imagine that you and your family are suddenly forced to cram your belongings into a handful of suitcases and flee your home, simply because of your religious beliefs or culture. Imagine that your parents are taken away and jailed because their political views differ from the views of those in power. And can you imagine what it would be like if you couldn't attend school because of your gender?

These are real examples of violations of human rights. Human rights laws protect people's rights to life, freedom, and equality. These laws are designed to unite the world community. They are universal, intended to apply to all people, and aim to prevent discrimination and to preserve human dignity.

In this chapter, we'll investigate how the concept of human rights evolved and how it has changed in response to specific circumstances. You'll also learn how, where, and why human rights continue to be violated, despite charters such as the UDHR.

What can you do to ensure that fundamental rights are guaranteed to all people? To start, let's take a look back at a moment in history when respect for human rights was at one of its lowest points.

LESSONS OF THE HOLOCAUST

In July 1938, the world's leaders turned their backs on Europe's Jewish community. It was in France, where delegates from 32 countries, including the United States, met to discuss Europe's growing number of Jewish asylum seekers.

The majority of the represented countries were unwilling to accept refugees, as they feared it would intensify the hardships of global economic depression. Only the Dominican Republic agreed to accept additional European refugees. At the end of the conference, the Intergovernmental Committee on Refugees (ICR) was established to monitor and address the situation.

At this time, German and Austrian Jews desperately sought safety from the anti-Semitic policies of the Nazi government of Adolf Hitler (1889–1945). These policies aimed to make life so difficult for Jewish residents that they would be forced into exile.

For those who did not escape, the Nazi policies eventually escalated to the Holocaust, which resulted in the state-sponsored persecution and murder of more than 6 million Jews. Other groups targeted by the Nazis included the Roma, people with disabilities, Slavic peoples, Jehovah's Witnesses, homosexuals, and political dissidents.

All told, more than
17 million people died in the Holocaust.

DIPLOMAT HELPERS

Many families reached Shanghai and other destinations in Asia thanks in part to the intervention of Chiune Sugihara (1900–1986) and Ho Feng Shan (1901–1997). Both served as diplomats during the 1930s and 1940s—Sugihara represented Japan in Lithuania and Shan represented China in Austria. Defying the orders of their superiors, these two men helped thousands of Jews escape Central and Eastern Europe at great personal cost. After leaving Lithuania, Sugihara and his family were interned for 18 months in a camp in the Soviet Union. On return to Japan after the war, he was asked to resign from the diplomatic service. The Holocaust remembrance organization Yad Vashem honored both men as "Righteous Among the Nations" for their aid to Jews fleeing Nazi persecution. Why do you think these people acted when no one else would?

HUMAN RIGHTS HISTORY

We often think of human rights as beginning at the time the UDHR was born, but in reality, more than 2,000 years of history led up to the creation of the UDHR. As complex societies emerged, so, too, did social divisions. In many early civilizations—and all the way to the present day—people with political and economic power have had rights and resources that they have tried to deny to everyone else. This kind of situation has always been a source of tension in society, whether in ancient Babylon, Colonial America, or twentieth-century India. The history of human rights is paved with the stories of people who addressed and continue to address this tension by rejecting the idea that only a privileged few should have rights.

Human rights—in the form best-known to citizens of our world—were formally outlined by the UN in 1948.

● ● ● ● ● ● ● ●

Because of immigration policies, fear, and the Great Depression, many countries refused to take any German immigrants. One of the few places in the world where Jews found sanctuary was in Shanghai, China, a "treaty port" that allowed foreigners to live, work, and trade in the city. By 1941, more than 20,000 refugees relocated to the city's Jewish quarter. This is where young Frances Flatow's parents met and married.

They both fled Germany in the late 1930s and early 1940s—her mother's family was among the last to receive exit visas in 1940. In Shanghai, the pair survived the Japanese occupation and being forced to live in a Jewish ghetto. They weathered the war, welcomed Frances in late 1947, and immigrated to the United States eight weeks later.

The family eventually settled in Providence, Rhode Island, alongside several other Shanghai Jewish families. Frances's father operated a gas station and her mother worked as a salesperson. Frances went to college, married, worked as a school guidance counselor, had two daughters, and, eventually, four grandchildren.

She remains mindful of her mother's narrow escape from genocide.

In 1948, the experience of refugee families such as the Flatows—as well as of the millions who failed to escape Europe—begged a series of crucial questions. How can we ensure that the rights of all people are protected and never again violated on this scale? How can we create a world in which intolerance isn't permitted and in which people seeking refuge can find it? These questions eventually led to the UDHR.

A committee of members representing Australia, Chile, France, the Soviet Union, the United Kingdom, China, France, Lebanon, and the United States, led by former U.S. First Lady Eleanor Roosevelt (1884–1962), drafted 30 essential and unalienable rights. What united the committee was a shared commitment to ending war, protecting people from violence, and ensuring that people who had caused no harm to others wouldn't be punished. Out of these ideas, the UDHR was born. It was formally adopted on December 10, 1948.

WHICH HUMAN RIGHTS?

"Human rights" is an umbrella term that covers two broad types of rights: political and social. Political rights address the powers and limits of governments and rulers. They also grant citizens the opportunity to freely participate in civic life and influence public policies. The UDHR spells out several rights that fall into this category, such as equality before the law and the right to assemble in public and protest.

Social rights center on the idea that governments should actively promote the well-being of their citizens. Economic, environmental, and cultural rights all fall under the grouping of social rights. These include the rights of workers, the right to education, and the right to leisure and play.

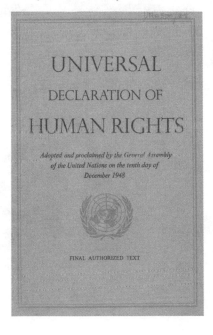

THE RIGHTS OF THE CHILD

Historically, kids haven't had a lot of rights. But during the past 100 years, human rights advocates have started paying attention to the unique rights of children. The Convention on the Rights of the Child aims to create a world in which children can develop their individual interests, talents, and identities. This document outlines what a child needs—including housing, education, health care, and food—to grow up healthy and thriving. This document applies to all children, regardless of race, ethnicity, family income, or religion. Approved in 1989, it guarantees children the following.

Provisions: the right to a name, good health, and a nationality.

Protections: safety from exploitation, detention, and removal from their family.

Participation: being entitled to have a voice in decisions that impact them.

This document is the most widely ratified in the world. All UN member states—except for the United States—have ratified it. You can read the document at this website. Why do you think the United States hasn't ratified? What are the two sides of the debate?

 rights of child

THE *CYRUS CYLINDER*

Many historians consider the *Cyrus Cylinder* to be the world's first document guaranteeing certain rights. In 539 BCE, Persian leader Cyrus the Great (601–530 BCE) conquered the city of Babylon. The *Cyrus Cylinder* informed the newly conquered Babylonians of their rights. This baked, clay cylinder freed enslaved people, allowed for religious liberty, and guaranteed equality among races and cultures in the city. While some experts argue about Cyrus's intentions and challenge the cylinder's status as the first human rights charter, it was certainly influential—leaders from Ancient Greece to Revolutionary-era America viewed it as a model of how to run a diverse empire.

 You can see the *Cyrus Cylinder* and read a translation of its words at this British Museum site.

 British Museum Cyrus Cylinder

All human rights overlap and interconnect. Consider the right to clean water—though it might be considered an environmental issue, political, economic, and cultural rights are part of this right.

A brief look at the UN's 30 fundamental rights shows just how interconnected they are.

1. We Are All Born Free and Equal
2. Freedom from Discrimination
3. The Right to Live in Freedom and Safety
4. Freedom From Slavery
5. Freedom From Torture
6. You Have Rights No Matter Where You Go
7. We're All Equal Before the Law
8. Your Human Rights Are Protected by Law
9. No Unfair Detainment
10. The Right to Fair Trial
11. We Are All Innocent Until Proven Guilty
12. The Right to Privacy

Children in Sindh, Pakistan, play at a water pump in a village.

Credit: The Department for International Development (CC BY 2.0)

13. Freedom to Move
14. The Right to Seek a Safe Place to Live
15. Right to a Nationality
16. Right to Marry and Found a Family
17. The Right to Own Property
18. Freedom of Thought
19. Freedom of Expression
20. The Right to Public Assembly
21. The Right to Democracy
22. Right to Health, Social Security, and Basic Needs
23. Workers' Rights
24. The Right to Play
25. Food and Shelter for All
26. The Right to Education
27. Right to Cultural Heritage
28. A Fair and Free World
29. Duty to Community
30. No One Can Take Away Your Human Rights

HUMAN RIGHTS HOTSPOTS

Every year, Human Rights Watch—an international nongovernmental organization (NGO)—issues a report identifying global human rights "hotspots." The map it publishes offers a window on some of these hotspots. Let's take a glance at snapshots of each hotspot, then we'll take a closer look in the following chapters.

Conditions change rapidly, especially in conflict zones. Use reputable current news sources to learn more about what's happening in each of these locations.

SANCTIONS

When diplomatic efforts fail to resolve conflict, countries and international bodies often impose sanctions instead of starting military action. Sanctions are economic penalties that block trade and transactions. They are designed to pressure countries that violate foreign- and security-policy norms. Sanctions can apply to entire governments and countries, such as North Korea, or can target specific businesses, groups, or individuals. The second option reduces the chances of civilians suffering from the actions of governments or corporations.

United States-Mexico Border—
Political, cultural, economic

The basics: Thousands of asylum seekers fleeing violence in Central America haven't had the chance to present their cases for resettlement in the United States. The U.S. government has separated thousands of children from their parents at the United States-Mexico border, leading observers to question whether the rights guaranteed to children in the UN Convention on the Rights of the Child were being violated. "Parties shall ensure that a child shall not be separated from his or her parents against their will, except when such separation is necessary for the best interests of the child."

The human toll: Refugees and asylum seekers have been turned away, facing violence and human rights violations in their home countries. According to Amnesty International, "approximately 8,000 family units were separated after crossing the border since 2017."

Venezuela—
Political, economical

The basics: For 20 years, Venezuela has been governed by leaders who disrespect democratic institutions. Other countries have reacted with sanctions, leaving the country on the brink of economic and political collapse.

The human toll: Venezuela's poverty rate stands at 82 percent. Residents lack access to basic necessities, including toilet paper, medicine, and food. Due to political and economic instability, more than 4.6 million people have left Venezuela. UN estimates hold that 6.5 million Venezuelans could be living outside of the country by the end of 2020, making it one of the largest mass displacements in modern history.

Syria—Political, cultural, economic

The basics: For eight years, civil war has ravaged Syria as rebel groups try to topple the military-supported government of Bashar al-Assad (1965–). Assad is still in power, and Syrian refugees have sought asylum across the planet.

The human toll: Hundreds of thousands of people have died as a result of bombings and chemical attacks. More than 5 million people have fled Syria, and an additional 6 million people had to flee their homes to another part of Syria.

Brazil—Environmental, political, cultural, economic

The basics: Brazilians in the Amazon region experience contamination of water, air, and soil as a result of poor environmental practices. The impact is both immediate and long-lasting, ranging from health effects on residents to large-scale biodiversity loss.

The human toll: Activists put themselves at great personal risk to protect land and communities. Millions of citizens are also at risk from contaminated soil and polluted air and water.

Cameroon—Political, cultural

The basics: In November 2016, lawyers, teachers, and students from Cameroon's English-speaking minority protested the lack of government representation and recognition by the country's French-speaking majority. The conflict between the two groups has grown increasingly violent, with atrocities committed on both sides.

The human toll: Countless villages have been burned and Cameroonians on both sides have been tortured and killed. In October 2019, estimates held that the conflict had resulted in 3,000 deaths, more than 500,000 displaced citizens, and 700,000 children without schooling.

BY THE HUMAN RIGHTS WATCH

Russia—Political, cultural

The basics: Free speech and expression are endangered in Russia. Disagreement with the government—whether through protests, art, music, or social media posts—can result in imprisonment.

The human toll: Public disagreement with the government can lead to arrest, fines, and imprisonment. For example, in late 2018 and early 2019, more than 40 people suspected of being gay were rounded up, detained, and tortured in Chechnya.

A 2018 protest in Russia

Yemen—Political, cultural, economic

The basics: The armed conflict in Yemen is based on political and religious differences between rebel Houthi forces and groups backed by the governments of Saudi Arabia and the United Arab Emirates. Restrictions on imports have led to dramatic price increases, food shortages, and international isolation.

The human toll: Since 2015, more than 17,500 civilians have been killed and injured. As a result of blockades and sanctions, more than 20 million people are food insecure and lack access to basic services, including healthcare. Ten million people are considered by the UN to be "one step away from famine." Today, the UN describes conditions in Yemen as the world's worst humanitarian crisis.

China—Political, cultural

The basics: Uighur Muslims in western China's Xinjiang state face cultural reprogramming in internment camps. Reports state that Uighurs are forced to learn Mandarin and criticize or renounce Islam.

The human toll: It is believed that up to 1 million Uighurs of Xinjiang's 11 million have been detained in government camps. Rights violations include physical and mental torture, all based on difference of belief and culture.

Myanmar (Burma)—Political, cultural

The basics: Ethnic and religious tensions have led the country's Buddhist majority to target Muslim Rohingya minorities. The military has led efforts to ethnically cleanse the country of Rohingya.

The human toll: Villages have been burned and rapes and state-sponsored killings have taken place across Myanmar's Rakine State. In addition, 700,000 Rohingya live in exile in neighboring Bangladesh.

North Korea—Political, cultural, economic

The basics: More than 100,000 political prisoners are held in North Korean prisons and forced labor camps. North Koreans can be arrested and detained for a variety of reasons, from making too much money to being caught trying to flee the country. Prisoners are forced to work, suffer near-starvation, and face harsh interrogations.

The human toll: In 2014, a UN Commission of Inquiry labeled North Korea's prison system a crime against humanity. It is currently estimated that about 120,000 North Koreans are being held in prison camps.

Philippines—Political, cultural

The basics: President Rodrigo Duterte's (1945–) ruthless "War on Drugs" has claimed the lives of thousands of Filipinos. Duterte has encouraged the murder of anyone suspected of selling or using drugs. Human rights watchdogs charge that the police frequently plant guns and other evidence to falsely justify executions. The regime has also targeted children living on the streets and petty criminals.

The human toll: While the official number of deaths hovers above 5,000, human rights groups believe that between 12,000 and 27,000 people have been murdered by death squads and militia groups.

WHO INTERVENES AND HOW?

History is filled with examples of defenders of human rights. Today's human rights activists continue this tradition. Individuals working with organizations such as the UN, Human Rights Watch, and Amnesty International strive to protect the rights of all people. They document violations, educate the public, develop policies to ensure compliance with international law, and intervene when conflicts arise.

It can be tempting to leave human rights work to the experts. It can also be easy to feel distant from events such as war, famine, disease, and drought that don't directly impact us. Often, these disasters take place somewhere far from us.

But in a global world, we are all interconnected. Humankind is bound together by the shared rights guaranteed in the UDHR and the UN Convention on the Rights of the Child.

> We owe it to one another to ensure
> that these rights are upheld.

You have the option to be more than simply a bystander and to act as an ally. No special qualifications are needed—simply educate yourself, inform others, and take action. What does action look like? You can raise funds, march in protests, organize boycotts, educate peers through articles and art, speak up against injustice, and consume responsibly. The possibilities are endless, and children worldwide are standing up to make positive change.

TRUTH TOLD

Between 1.5 and 2 million Venezuelans have fled to neighboring Colombia. In total, more than 5 million refugees and migrants have fled Venezuela, seeking safety and protection elsewhere in the world. This has created the largest mass displacement in Latin American history. In May 2020, 60 countries participating in the International Donors Conference in Solidarity with Venezuelan Refugees and Migrants in Latin America and the Caribbean pledged $2.79 billion in aid to address critical needs of refugees amid the COVID-19 pandemic.

THINK GLOBALLY, ACT LOCALLY

Schools are little worlds all of their own. There's a good chance that some of the challenges to human dignity that present themselves globally will pop up in your learning community.

As conversations about human rights expand, you might have the chance to teach your teacher and peers about topics such as gender identity, bullying, and racial discrimination. In some instances, you may be advocating for yourself. At other times, you might be an ally for classmates facing discrimination.

What can you do to create a safe school community in which everyone feels recognized? Here are some ways people help defend human rights in local communities.

Schoolchildren march for climate action in Melbourne, Australia, 2018.

Credit: Julian Meehan (CC BY 2.0)

Read more about
Mix It Up at Lunch
days on the Teaching
Tolerance website.

 tolerance mix
it up

A celebration of the twenty-first
anniversary of the UN Convention on Rights
of the Child, November 19, 2010, in Wales

Credit: National Assembly for Wales (CC BY 2.0)

- Gender (UN SDGs 5, 10, 16): Not everyone identifies with the labels of "male" or "female" as assigned at birth. In a recent survey in Minnesota, 2.7 percent of youth responded as gender nonconforming, or nonbinary. In many schools, students in Gay-Straight Alliances (GSAs) help others in the community understand the impact of their gender assumptions. GSA activists might take actions to make their communities more inclusive, such as advocating for gender-neutral bathrooms, including categories beyond male or female on school forms, and educating others about the use of gender-neutral pronouns such as "ze" or "they."

- Bullying (UN SDGs 3, 4, 16): Each year, one in five students reports being bullied at school. Bullies often target those considered different because of their race, religion, abilities, gender identity, or immigration status. Estimates are that 75 percent of bullying results from bias. Join other students in creating a culture at your school in which students aren't singled out. Speak out when someone is being mistreated. Organize a Mix It Up at Lunch Day, which encourages students to meet new people by sitting with and talking to different people in the cafeteria. You can speak out against injustice and break down barriers, divisions, and misunderstandings.

- Racial discrimination (UN SDGs 3, 10, 16): From unequal punishment to textbooks that leave out certain historical events, racial discrimination happens in schools. This impacts how and what kids learn. Through petitions and proposals, you can be a student activist to change what's taught and to ensure that everyone is represented.

> Encourage open and honest conversation on racism in your school community to ensure that the human rights of all students are upheld.

PROFILES IN GLOBAL CITIZENSHIP

Zunera Gilani
Location: Around the world
Job Title: Epidemiologist

Every day, Zunera Gilani works to make SDG 3—"Good Health and Well-Being"—a closer reality for people across the globe. Gilani is an epidemiologist who works with ministries

Credit: courtesy of Zunera Gilani

of health on multiple continents to carry out vaccination programs.

In 2018, Gilani traveled on 114 separate planes to Uganda, Jordan, France, Kenya (four times), England, Papua New Guinea, Australia, and Pakistan. In the spring of 2020, her focus shifted from international to domestic work as she volunteered with COVID-19 response efforts in the United States.

How did she get interested in this work?

From the age of nine to 22, Gilani wanted to be an archaeologist. She even earned an undergraduate degree in classics and pursued a master's in Near Eastern art and archaeology. But her interests shifted when she went to Pakistan with her twin sister to assist with public health fieldwork.

Due to vaccine hesitancy—the reluctance or refusal to vaccinate even when vaccines are readily available—global measles cases increased 30 percent from 2016 to 2017.

A RACE AGAINST TIME

Vaccines usually take years to research, develop, and test, but scientists around the world fast-tracked their efforts to produce a vaccine for COVID-19, which, as of early June 2020, had killed more than 400,000 people worldwide. Some researchers believe a vaccine will be available by early 2021. Then, the world will tackle the problem of getting the vaccine to as many people as possible. Most world leaders agree that governments, banking institutions, nonprofit groups, and research organizations need to work together to ensure the vaccine is affordable for even the poorest populations. The aid group Doctors Without Borders has recommended that the vaccine be sold at cost—meaning, without profit.

Gilani explains, "This experience, which involved interviewing mothers, completely reshaped my path. I loved the process of doing fieldwork, specifically something that was scientifically structured but that allowed me to interact with people who I normally wouldn't meet."

"Doing something so current—having to do with the here and now—was really transformative."

What steps did she take to get where she is?

Gilani knew that she wanted to work in global public health, with an emphasis on infectious disease. She explains that there were some barriers to entering this type of work. "To do global public health work, you need a lot of field experience. Most internships that offer this type of experience are unpaid. I interned with the Texas State Department of Health in Austin and got my first job as epidemiologist with the Texas Department of Public Health. Through that experience, I learned how health systems work and gathered methods for working with different types of public health programs.

"After that, I took an unpaid internship with the World Health Organization (WHO) in Pakistan. I worked on a polio eradication campaign, and that turned into a paid job. My supervisor had an interesting perspective on polio, treating it as an entity that you had to track, focusing on figuring out what it wants to do in order to root it out. I took that experience and enrolled in a PhD program, knowing that I wanted to return to this type of work after finishing my degree."

What's the best part of her job?

Gilani finds field experience the best part of her job. "Collecting data and monitoring a program," she explains, "is such a unique experience. I feel so grateful when I interact with health care workers who are so dedicated and who sacrifice so much to provide services to underserved people. That's when I really feel the work is meaningful."

What are some pressing global health concerns and exciting developments in global public health?

"The WHO notes that vaccine hesitancy is a big threat to global public health," Gilani explains. "We have all the tools to control diseases, but they're not always being used."

Despite these challenges, developments in global public health keep her motivated. "We are on the cusp of eradicating polio and measles," she elaborates. "These are big goals, but having them are really motivating because they can strengthen health systems in general. Currently, smallpox is the only disease that's been fully eradicated. It's exciting to think that we can use education and public health tools to eliminate these diseases in our lifetimes."

In the next chapter, we'll dive into learning about human rights and global citizenship through the lens of politics. There's a lot going on in global politics that touches many aspects of our lives!

STAY HEALTHY

In 2017, 6.3 million children under the age of 17 died. More than half of these deaths were preventable. According to UN International Children's Emergency Fund (UNICEF), the primary killers of children in the developing world are pneumonia, diarrhea, malaria, measles, HIV/AIDS, and malnutrition. Organizations such as the U.S. Centers for Disease Control, the WHO, and UNICEF work to eliminate or control these causes of death through vaccines, health services, proper sanitation, and good nutrition. Why is health considered a human right?

TEXT TO WORLD

How can you work to protect human rights in your everyday life?

KEY QUESTIONS

- Why do human rights laws exist? What rights do they protect?
- What twentieth-century events led to the development of the UDHR?
- What human rights challenges exist in today's world?

VOCAB LAB 📖

Write down what you think each word means. What root words can you find to help you? What does the context of the word tell you?

advocate, **bias**, **discrimination**, **equality**, **gender identity**, **humanitarian**, **injustice**, **refugee**, and **sanction**.

Compare your definitions with those of your friends or classmates. Did you all come up with the same meanings? Turn to the text and glossary if you need help.

ACTING ON THE SUSTAINABLE DEVELOPMENT GOALS

The UN SDGs were designed to prompt action in response to pressing global concerns. The 17 SDGs aim to create a better world by addressing challenges that face the communities to which we all belong—local, national, and international.

In this activity, you'll relate the SDGs to human rights issues in your local community.

* **Review the 17 SDGs on page 4.** Keeping them in mind, look at local newspapers and websites to find human rights topics that impact your community. Look for stories that relate to the categories of poverty, health, education, equality, peace/personal safety, and the environment. Which are reflected in local and state news?

* **Create a table with the six categories noted above.** Map the "Who, What, When, Where, and Why" of the stories you find.

* **Choose one issue.** Research what is being done about it in your community. What organizations are addressing it and how? How can you get involved in making change?

* **Reach out to the organization's leadership.** Invite them to visit your class or club, either remotely or in person. Discuss ways that you can collaborate to create positive change and develop a step-by-step plan for action.

	Poverty	Health	Education	Equality	Peace and Safety	Environment
Who is involved in the story or event?						
Which SDG are people addressing?						
When did the event or story take place? What is the history behind it?						
Where did it happen? Did it just impact your community?						
Why is this a challenge or problem?						
How are people addressing it?						

To investigate more, visit the UN-created resource, "170 Daily Actions to Transform Our World." Which of these direct and actionable tips can you implement in your communities?

🔍 UN 170 actions

TRUTH TOLD

Due to stay-at-home orders and lockdowns, routine childhood immunization rates plummeted during the COVID-19 pandemic. WHO experts warned that this disruption to infant vaccinations put 80 million babies worldwide at risk of preventable illnesses such as measles.

WHAT ARE VACCINES?

According to the WHO, vaccines prevent 2 to 3 million deaths per year. Another 1.5 million deaths globally could be avoided with improved vaccine coverage. Access to immunization for all people on the planet is critical to meeting SDG 3, "Good Health and Well-being." What does that mean in today's world?

* **Using the websites of the WHO and CDC, research the following.**

  * How do vaccines work?

  * What are the phases of vaccine development?

  * Who develops vaccines? Who coordinates these efforts?

  * How long does it typically take to develop a vaccine?

  * Can the vaccine development process be accelerated? What does that mean for COVID-19?

* **Investigate how previous vaccines—notably, the measles vaccine—work.** Look for statistics on measles cases and deaths by year. Make a chart that shows how this vaccine has led to a reduction in global measles cases and deaths.

To investigate more, make an infographic explaining what goes into creating vaccines and why they matter for healthy communities. Include details about how vaccine availability creates other opportunities, especially in areas such as access to education.

Chapter 2 ▶

Your Political Rights

YOU HAVE A VOICE IN THE POLITICAL PROCESS REGARDLESS OF YOUR AGE. SPEAK OUT ON ISSUES IMPACTING YOUR COMMUNITY!

How can you exercise your political and civil rights to improve the world?

You might associate politics with campaigns for public office, voting booths, and official debates. But politics is much more than this. In fact, politics means "of, for, or relating to citizens." When thought of this way, politics is about community dialogue and informed action. It's about having a voice and making that voice heard.

● ● ● ● ● ● ●

You might think that political action belongs just to city council members or congresspeople or UN delegates—but it is the right and responsibility of all people. And the good news is that you can get politically involved and take political action in many ways. You don't have to be old enough to vote or serve as an elected official to be political or to express opinions.

As a young person, you have every right to speak out on issues impacting your community, just like countless other youth worldwide.

Across time and on every continent, people have fought for political rights in order to ensure their individual liberties and to set limits on the power of government. In their current form, these rights give citizens a way to express thoughts and opinions and to shape laws.

While political rights and civil liberties vary by nation, the UDHR identifies the following fundamental rights and liberties:

- Freedom of movement

- Equality before the law

- The right to a fair trial; innocence until proven guilty

- Freedom of thought, conscience, and religion

- Freedom of opinion and expression

- The right to peaceful assembly and free association

- Participation in public affairs and elections

- Protection of minority rights

- Privacy

These rights also guarantee that people cannot be subjected to the following conditions.

- Deprived of life, or tortured and subject to cruel or degrading treatment or punishment

- Enslaved or forced into labor

- Arrested or detained without reason

- Subjected to war propaganda

- Targeted by discrimination

- Subjected to racial or religious hatred

DISPATCHES FROM SYRIA

Let's look at these political rights from a personal point of view. What is it like to fight for what you believe in? How can people fight for civil liberties, both for themselves and others?

FREEDOM OF EXPRESSION

If you live in a country such as the United States or Australia or Great Britain, you probably take for granted that you can express yourself politically. But that's not true for people who live in countries such as China, North Korea, or even Russia. In these countries, freedom of speech and expression are restricted, the media is controlled by the state, and governments routinely monitor online and offline behavior.

For citizens in speech-restricted environments, each text, email, or public expression is crafted with the knowledge that it could be watched by officials. If the views relayed are critical of the government, it could even result in harsh penalties or arrest.

THE SYRIAN CIVIL WAR

More than 400,000 Syrians have died since that country's civil war began in 2011. Additionally, more than 5.6 million Syrians have fled the country and 6 million people are displaced from their homes within the country's borders. The conflict began during the anti-authoritarian protests of the Arab Spring, when people marched and protested against governments across the Muslim world. That's when Syrian President Bashar al-Assad arrested and imprisoned 15 boys who were supportive of democratic reform. One boy died while detained. Citizen-led protests erupted and hundreds of activists were killed.

In the summer of that year, a rebel group called the Free Syrian Army formed to challenge Assad's power. In the course of the conflict, the terrorist group ISIS also tried to seize territory within Syria. As of 2020, Assad's regime remains intact and the conflict and violence continue.

"The humanitarian and medical crisis in Eastern Ghouta is difficult to describe with words," explained Syrian teen Muhammad Najem to the Turkish Radio and Television network. Since 2017, Najem has used video to show the global community what words fail to express about the human toll of the Syrian civil war, a conflict stemming from the suppression of people's political and civil rights.

Credit: Christiaan Triebert (CC BY 2.0)

Using social media such as Twitter, Facebook, and YouTube, Najem documents life during wartime, focusing on the human side of a political conflict. In some videos, common, everyday actions—three children passing a soccer ball back and forth—are set against uncommon backdrops, such as the rubble of destroyed buildings.

Other posts highlight horrible realities, such as showing a starving 63-year-old man in desperate need of medical attention. In another, a little boy whose leg was amputated after a bombing sends a message to his favorite soccer star. Next to him stands a friend whose face was severely scarred in a chemical weapons attack.

Najem's efforts to draw awareness to the conflict have attracted worldwide attention. He's been featured on television programs in Turkey, France, and Brazil.

Global coverage of these atrocities is his intent. In one video, Najem says directly and pointedly at the camera, "We are killed by your silence." He uses social media to connect with people across the planet, calling upon them to uphold their responsibilities to defend the political and civil rights guaranteed to all people, regardless of geography.

What are the political and civil rights that bind all global citizens?

What are their origins and how have they evolved? Why do some governments continue to refuse to recognize them? And what can you do to guarantee that they are upheld?

A HISTORICAL LOOK

Historically, not all people have enjoyed equal access to political and civil rights. The late 1700s and early 1800s witnessed revolutionary movements toward independence in the United States, France, Haiti, Venezuela, and elsewhere. People rejected monarchies and demanded the right to self-government.

In all these settings, women and non-Europeans contributed to this fight. Yet these new governments generally limited the right to vote and participate in politics to men of European ancestry. In early U.S. history, most states allowed only land-owning, white men to vote and govern. Women and people of color were excluded. Does that sound fair to you?

Watch this video from Najem. What makes it so powerful? Can you imagine living in a place where bombing happened every day?

🔍 Muhammad Najem birds

WHO'S IN CHARGE?

Enforcing the promises made in the UDHR falls to national governments. Governments set their own rules and policies, based on their unique histories, cultures, and context. When individual political rights are violated, people can seek justice through court systems. Judges carefully weigh arguments to reach a verdict, or decision, in each case. In the United States, cases involving political and civil rights sometimes end up before the U.S. Supreme Court. International legal institutions also exist to protect and enforce political and civil rights. Regional courts such as the Inter-American Court of Human Rights address regional conflicts. The UN's International Court of Justice resolves political conflicts between UN member states. A separate body, the International Criminal Court, prosecutes leaders accused of violating human rights. In theory, many levels of security are in place to ensure people are protected and supported.

SAUDI ARABIA

In June 2018, Saudi women were granted the right to drive. But that doesn't mean that women in Saudi Arabia now enjoy total and complete freedom. Women still cannot open a bank account, get a passport, travel abroad, or get married or divorced without the permission of a man. Single women and men sit in separate sections in coffee shops and restaurants, and women's dress is expected to cover the body from head-to-toe.

Suffragists fought a decades-long battle to win women's voting rights.

Without the political and civil rights of full citizenship, women and people of color couldn't shape the laws and rules that impacted them. Basic rights such as privacy, the right to a fair trial, and freedom of expression were denied to these groups. So, people formed groups within civil society to use their voices to change this. Often, these individuals corresponded and collaborated—sometimes across oceans—in order to achieve social change.

Key social movements of the past two centuries that fought for more inclusive political and civil rights include the following.

Abolitionism

This eighteenth- and nineteenth-century movement fought to end slavery and establish political rights and representation for enslaved peoples.

Women's movements/suffrage

This nineteenth- and twentieth-century movement worked for equal rights and protections under law for women and focused on property and voting rights.

Anti-colonial movements

Various twentieth-century movements across Africa and Asia sought to free their countries from European colonization and establish independence and self-governance.

Civil rights movements

Mid-twentieth-century movements, especially powerful in the United States, aimed to hold governments true to the promise of full equality for minority groups.

New social movements

Within these movements that gained traction in the mid- to late-twentieth century, groups of activists including women, LGBTQ, and peace advocates worked on issues of identity and the right to publicly express it.

Demonstration of Mothers of the Plaza de Mayo, December 2010, Argentina
Credit: David Berkowitz (CC BY 2.0)

REUNITING FAMILIES

From 1976 to 1983, between 10,000 and 30,000 activists who opposed Argentina's military government disappeared. They were kidnapped by the government. Basic political and civil rights—freedom of speech, the right to assemble, and freedom of opinion—were violated on a mass scale. Some of the kidnapped activists were pregnant. These women were held in detention until they gave birth, at which time their children were taken and given up for adoption to families that supported the government. Then, their mothers were killed. Family members of these "desaparecidos"—the disappeared— refused to stop searching for their children and grandchildren. Through regular, silent protest, they confronted the military's abuses and demanded justice. As of 2017, 127 children of the disappeared have been reunited with family members, largely thanks to DNA testing.

Activists in all these social movements endured brutality, arrest, violence, and intimidation to lay the groundwork for the political rights and civil liberties that many people enjoy today.

Unfortunately, many of these struggles remain unresolved.

The UN SDGs point to the continued need for improvement, particularly in areas such as gender and racial equality, the right to decent work and economic growth, and the need to build peace, justice, and strong institutions.

WHY REPRESSION?

You might think that one of the main purposes of a government is to care for and protect its citizens. But, often in an effort to maintain power, many political, economic, religious, social, and intellectual reasons lead governments to suppress human rights. State-sponsored violence can take different physical and non-physical forms, including psychological and emotional, all of which is designed to incite fear, terror, and submission.

Physical suppression often involves the military or police. Autocrats who want to maintain power, such as Assad in Syria, use force to try to silence the opposition and keep dissenting views from public debates.

Pro-democracy protesters in Hong Kong brave heavy rain as they march on August 18, 2019. Demonstrations began in April 2019 over a proposed bill that gave China the power to extradite criminal suspects to the mainland.

Credit: Studio Incendo (CC BY 2.0)

This can translate into the arrests and beatings of protesters, raids on opposition group meetings, bombing campaigns, imprisonment, torture, and full-fledged civil war between those in power and those who challenge their authority.

Non-physical violence often targets specific populations, such as minority groups, women, and the poor.

> Historically, racist policies such as poll taxes and literacy tests in the United States were designed to keep entire groups of people from voting.

This is what happened with Jim Crow laws that structured race relations from 1877 until the mid-twentieth century. These laws made segregation legal, rolling back the racial progress made during Reconstruction (1863–1877). Under Jim Crow, African Americans were often kept from voting by tests they couldn't pass and taxes that they couldn't pay.

Some critics argue that today's voter identification laws in some parts of the United States aim to achieve the same thing, making it harder for black, Asian, Latinx, young, and poor people to participate in elections. We see this by way of mass incarceration, which disproportionately affects people of color, who are then denied the right to vote even after they serve their sentence.

This isn't a problem just in the United States. Similar measures to prevent alleged voter fraud by requiring identification have been proposed in the United Kingdom and France.

Governments sometimes go to great lengths to stifle political rights and civil liberties.

FIXING LAW ENFORCEMENT IN THE UNITED STATES

After a rash of high-profile cases shone a spotlight on systemic racism and police brutality in early 2020, a number of activists called for major change to policing in the United States. Some called for extensive reform, while others pushed to defund and dismantle police forces. Additional voices argued for the total abolition of policing and a reimagination of law enforcement. What arguments can be marshalled in favor of each?

Did you know there's a National Voter Registration Day? It's the fourth Tuesday of every September!

Credit: League of Women Voters (CC BY 2.0)

TRUTH TOLD

Women make up the majority of migrants in Europe and the Americas.

Questions about political rights, civil liberties, and whether certain government actions are repressive are often hotly debated. For example, in the United States after 9/11, fears about terrorism led to the passage of the Patriot Act. This legislation allowed the government to wiretap civilian phone lines, leading to major concerns about privacy and racial profiling. It also launched debates about the weight given to national security over individual liberties.

Should the government be allowed to listen to private conversations among citizens? Why or why not? People continue to argue over these questions.

THINK GLOBALLY, ACT LOCALLY

It can be difficult to wrap your head around the idea of taking global political action—it's such an overwhelming thought! Here's the good news. Think back to the UN SDGs on page 4. Each of those global goals can be enacted on different scales, or levels, including locally. Here are some issues related to SDG 16, which covers building "Peace, Justice and Strong Institutions." How are these being addressed in your community?

Asylum seekers

Political conflict, police corruption, denial of civil liberties, and violence in places such as Honduras, Syria, and Afghanistan drive citizens to move elsewhere in search of asylum. In many places where gender-based violence is common, women and LGBTQ individuals flee because their governments fail to protect them from personal violence. Even their lives might be in danger.

These refugees are pursuing their fundamental rights to freedom and safety.

Locally

Young people are bridging divides and helping new immigrants and refugees settle into their local communities. In Pittsburgh, Pennsylvania, high schooler Peyton Klein launched an afterschool program called Global Minds Initiative.

> Global Minds combats intolerance and discrimination by pairing students who are native English speakers with English language learners (ELL).

This offers the ELL students educational support and enables all students to learn about each other's cultures. Global Minds also sponsors community events such as dinners, field trips, and speakers to broaden understanding of the political, social, and economic factors that lead people to seek asylum.

Today, Global Minds has 23 chapters, with more than 1,000 participating students. You can grow the network by launching one at your school!

Nationally and Globally

The flow of migrants constantly changes due to events and other circumstances. Government policies are not always responsive to these shifts. Although the world has changed dramatically during the past 20 years, the United States has had the same immigration laws since 1996.

Research your country's policies, particularly around refugees and asylum seekers. Are your government's laws and actions consistent with the UDHR? What is being done to build peace, justice, and strong institutions in the home countries of refugees? Reach out to immigration attorneys and activists. Invite them to your school to discuss how you can help.

Listen to Peyton Klein describe how she came to act locally to make a difference in her school.

 come sit with me

CITY OF SANCTUARY

In many parts of the world, entire communities are trying to address refugee and immigration issues. In the United Kingdom and Northern Ireland, 80-plus villages, towns, cities, and regions participate in the City of Sanctuary network. The people who participate in the network aim to build understanding by allowing all residents to feel visible, welcomed, and valued. Do some research to see if similar efforts exist in your area. You could be a pioneer in launching something similar in your town!

PUSH AND PULL

A combination of push and pull factors drive human migration. Push factors such as political conflict, disasters, and poor economic and educational prospects cause people to leave a community. In contemporary Honduras, for example, gender-based violence and threats to physical safety are major factors pushing women and children out of the country. Pull factors draw people to a new community. These factors include the promise of political and civil freedoms, a better climate, and improved economic and educational opportunities. What pull factors might draw people to your town?

During periods of crisis, xenophobia often surges as people look to place blame on scapegoats. The COVID-19 pandemic proved no different.

In May 2020, UN Secretary-General António Guterres denounced the "tsunami" of hate speech and scare-mongering erupting during the COVID-19 outbreak.

JUSTICE AND FREEDOM FROM DISCRIMINATION

All people have the right to equality before the law and to a fair trial. People also have the right not to be arrested or detained without reason. Unfortunately, these fundamental rights aren't always respected. In some settings, they are unevenly applied based on factors such as race, ethnicity, social class, and beliefs.

For example, "stop-and-frisk" policies in New York City, which permit police to stop, detain, question, and search civilians, overwhelmingly target black and Latinx individuals. According to the New York Civil Liberties Union, "Between 2014 and 2017, young black and Latino males between the ages of 14 and 24 account for only 5 percent of the city's population, compared with 38 percent of reported stops. Young black and Latino males were innocent 80 percent of the time." How can you help make the justice system more just?

Locally

Explore juvenile justice issues in your city and state. Youth incarceration has an effect on the well-being of individuals and communities, now and in the future.

Research shows that in the United States, despite similar crime rates, black adolescents are incarcerated at five times the rate of their white peers. What can you do to help ensure that the rights to equality before the law are respected in your community?

In Chicago, Illinois, youth advocates serving on the Mikva Challenge Juvenile Justice Council worked with the county board and judicial advisory council to build an app that allows formerly incarcerated youth to see if their records can be wiped clean. The app also connects youth in the juvenile justice system with attorneys willing to help them remove their criminal records. This gives kids another chance to pursue opportunities that might otherwise be unavailable to them due to having criminal records.

> In other communities, restorative justice—sometimes called transformative justice—offers an alternative to jail for young offenders.

This practice allows a young person who has committed a minor crime to sit down and discuss their actions with the people their crime affected and with other members of their community. They then develop a plan for making amends.

Youth courts, in which offenders appear before a panel of peers that issues a sentencing decision, also provide an effective forum for addressing minor offenses. Sentencing options include community service, written apologies, essays, and educational workshops. More than 1,050 youth courts are currently in operation in the United States—in towns, counties, and cities of all sizes.

Visit the National Association of Youth Courts website to see if your community has a restorative justice program.

 National Youth Courts

TRUTH TOLD

Recidivism is repeating criminal behavior and being rearrested. Follow-up studies show recidivism rates of between 6 and 9 percent for restorative justice and youth court programs. Compare that to recidivism rates of up to 76 percent for youth held in detention facilities.

Nationally and Globally

Around the world, people can be detained or arrested simply because their race, ethnicity, sexual orientation, social class, or thoughts differ from those in power. For example, in countries such as China, Egypt, Saudi Arabia, Venezuela, Honduras, and Turkey, reporters have been arrested, detained, and even murdered because of their work, particularly about politics and human rights.

Organizations such as the Committee to Protect Journalists advocate for imprisoned journalists and work to preserve free speech and information. Why is it crucial that journalists be allowed to do their jobs?

VOTING RIGHTS AND REPRESENTATION

In most countries, the legal voting age is 18. But you can exercise influence over elections and politics before you can vote! You can have a voice in the political process, regardless of your age.

Locally

As a young person, you are entitled to represent yourself in discussions of issues that directly impact your life. Whether through serving on a student council, being a student representative to a school board or city council, working on political campaigns, or delivering your perspective on policies to a state legislature, your voice can and should be heard.

Around the world, students have worked to take part in decision-making processes. They have achieved everything from reforms to the school dress code to revisions of city curfews.

A student council meets with the Maryland Lt. Gov. Boyd Rutherford in Baltimore, Maryland.

Credit: Maryland GovPics (CC BY 2.0)

At the local and state level, young people have appeared before lawmakers to speak about how issues such as gun violence have affected their lives. In U.S. states such as Maryland and Florida, youth activists have brought about concrete, legal changes related to gun reform.

Students at Marjory Stoneman Douglas High School in Florida responded to a February 2018 school shooting that claimed the lives of 17 people with the collective cry of "Never Again." Their work organizing the March for Our Lives in Washington, DC, later that year changed the national dialogue about gun violence. They've also spurred lawmakers in Florida and elsewhere to adopt measures to prevent future mass shootings.

Listen to Emma Gonzalez's speech at the March for Our Lives. Do you find this speech powerful? Why?

Emma Gonzalez speech Guardian

TRUTH TOLD

Rwanda has the highest number of women serving in public office. Women occupy 61.3 percent of seats in the lower house of Parliament.

CONNECT WITH GLOBAL PEERS

Many organizations help politically active youth around the globe connect with one another. Events such as the UN International Youth Day, held each August, encourage young people around the world to think about and enact global solutions to global challenges.

The UN International Youth Day website includes a toolkit for hosting events that range from community cleanups to concerts, as well as tips for drawing attention to youth issues and promoting political engagement. Other avenues to explore include conferences that bring young people from around the world together to explore political issues. The annual Critical Issues Forum brings teens from the United States, Japan, and Russia together to discuss strategies for the disarmament of nuclear weapons and for global security.

Nationally and Globally

Many of the local actions that you can take—investigating policies, petitioning, and lobbying for change—also apply nationally and globally. Here are some steps you can take.

- Research the positions of your elected officials on human rights issues that affect people across borders.

- Campaign for candidates who advocate for the political and civil rights of all people.

- Educate your family and friends on political and civil rights issues. Encourage them to vote.

- Use mock elections at your school to profile national and global concerns about political and civil rights. Engage your peers in dialogue about these rights.

PROFILES IN GLOBAL CITIZENSHIP

Michael Edison Hayden
Location: Undisclosed
Job Title: Senior Investigative Reporter, *Hatewatch*

Credit: courtesy of Michael Edison Hayden

Mike Hayden's journalism career took an unexpected turn on August 12, 2017. At the time, he worked for ABC News. A colleague needed the weekend off, and Hayden covered their shift. That Saturday, white supremacists rallied in Charlottesville, Virginia. The event quickly turned violent, as extremists clashed with anti-racism activists. It turned fatal when a man who was part of a neo-Nazi group drove a car into a crowd of protesters, killing activist Heather Heyer (1985–2017).

During the next several weeks, Hayden covered events as they developed. "I wanted to report on the leaders of the movement aggressively, with intense scrutiny," he explains. "I wanted to make sure that what happened at Charlottesville would never happen again."

Hayden moved from ABC to *Newsweek*, and in 2018, he joined *Hatewatch* at the Southern Poverty Law Center, an organization with the mission of pushing hate to the fringes of society. At *Hatewatch*, he's covered topics ranging from the forces that shape U.S. immigration policy to the exploitation of COVID-19 by alt-right extremist groups.

Hayden discusses his work and its bearing on "Peace, Justice, and Strong Institutions" (SDG 16).

What steps did he take to reach his position?

Hayden's original intention wasn't to be a reporter— he planned to be a playwright. "I picked up journalism while living in India as a way to pay the rent," he recalls. "I covered a lot of subjects in Southeast Asia, including the 2015 Nepal earthquake."

After several years abroad, Hayden returned to the United States, where he covered mainstream news. Following Charlottesville, he shifted to writing about extremism. He notes that his unconventional background equipped him with a different skill set than trained journalists.

"Many mainstream reporters struggle with these subjects. The players in supremacist and extremist movements lie to the media and manipulate reporters to get their message out. They threaten. They chase reporters online. They try to spread disinformation. My outsider experience helped me adapt to the tricky nature of the material more easily than I would have if I took a different path."

The Southern Poverty Law Center tracked hate groups across the country and mapped them in 2018. You can see the map at this website. What makes maps useful when doing research on culture and politics?

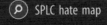 SPLC hate map

How does his work reinforce human dignity?

"When a person scapegoats another person based on their race, religion, or sexuality, there's injustice," Hayden notes. "When scapegoating involves using fake science to demean non-white people, there's injustice. When white supremacists organize to terrorize people with violence, there's injustice."

Hayden sees parallels between what's happening in the United States and elsewhere. "White supremacy is a problem in America but this is a global movement, not unlike what you see from terror groups such as ISIS. Every story we do has an international component, due to the terroristic values white supremacists hold."

In late May 2020, the homicide of George Floyd at the hands of four Minneapolis police officers sparked outrage in and beyond the United States. Activists continue to push for an end to violence and institutional racism through organized protests and social movement networks such as #BlackLivesMatter.

Credit: Julian Wan on Unsplash

On what social and political issues should readers educate themselves?

"The first step in fighting back is to be aware of what extremists believe, why they believe it, and what they plan to do to society," Hayden advises.

He continues, "Learn about male supremacy, which falsely blames women for the unhappiness of men. Learn about how white supremacists scapegoat Jewish people, falsely portraying them as puppet-masters out to hurt Christians. Learn about how bigots use fear of change to condemn LGBTQ people for being different from them. Learn about how racists use junk science to dehumanize non-whites. Learn how white supremacists use economic fears to blame immigrants for things they have nothing to do with.

"The more you know about organized bigots and how they think, the easier it is to reject them wherever they pop up," he says. "The best bulwark in the fight against hate is the ability to see it, recognize it, and to call it out for what it is with passion."

It's vital to consider human rights from many different directions. Now that you know more about the political aspect, let's turn our view to the economic side.

VOCAB LAB

Write down what you think each word means. What root words can you find to help you? What does the context of the word tell you?

autocrat, **civil liberties**, **dissent**, **disinformation**, **extremism**, **intolerance**, **migrant**, **repressive**, and **scapegoat**.

Compare your definitions with those of your friends or classmates. Did you all come up with the same meanings? Turn to the text and glossary if you need help.

KEY QUESTIONS

- In the case of the U.S. Patriot Act, the right to privacy and the right to live free from terror stand in conflict. Why might one right be protected over the other? How could both rights be honored?

- What is civil society? How have organizations in civil society reshaped political and civil rights laws throughout history?

TEXT TO WORLD

What community issues do you care most about? How do these local issues relate to the global issues you care about?

LEARN FROM THE PAST

Researchers who study past social movements discover the conditions that allowed for their success. Some researchers believe that activists need certain resources to build an organization. The five types of resources are:

- **Material: Money and physical resources for things such as brochures and transportation**

- **Moral: A sense of connection between members and moral support for goals**

- **Social-Organizational: Networks of partners, allies, and supporters, as well as previous organizing experience**

- **Human: Volunteers, leaders, and staff to campaign for the issue**

- **Cultural: Experience working in activist networks and knowledge of issues**

To investigate more, choose a contemporary political movement to research. Possibilities include the Dakota Access Pipeline protests, "Arab Spring," Youth for Climate Action, Black Lives Matter, or an immigrant rights movement. Consider the resources that activists use to reach local, national, and global audiences. How do this movement's tactics and strategies mirror your historical example? How do they differ? What is social media's role in the movement?

- **Choose a social movement mentioned earlier in the chapter.** Research and consider the following factors.

  - Who were the key figures in this movement?

  - What were some key turning points? How did the movement use this turning point to its advantage, and how did public opinion change as a result?

  - How did leaders of this movement use the media (newspapers, television, radio, the internet) to draw attention to their cause?

- **Create a chart outlining the five resource areas that activists use—material, moral, social-organizational, human, and cultural.** Map the social movement that you selected on this chart.

HOW OLD TO ROCK THE VOTE?

Around the world, the average age at which people can start voting ranges from 16 to 25 years of age. Is there a right age for people to participate in electoral politics?

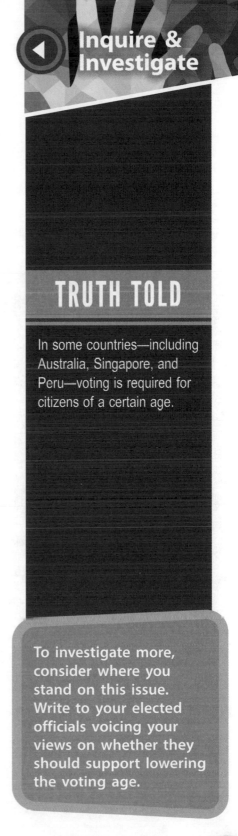

Inquire & Investigate

- **What's the national voting age in your country?** What's the voting age for local elections in your community? Is there currently debate about whether this age should change?

- **Investigate the legal voting age in other parts of the world.** What is the legal age and when was it set? What groups advocated for and against it? Did this impact outcomes of elections?

- **Countries you may want to consider include:**

· Argentina	· Italy	· Scotland
· Austria	· Japan	· United States
· Brazil	· Lebanon	· Ethiopia
· Iran	· Nicaragua	· Cameroon

- **Research arguments for and against lowering the voting age.**

  - What claims are made by people who want to lower the voting age? What claims are made by those who oppose it?

  - What evidence does each side use to support its claim?

  - What arguments could be made to weaken the claims of both sides? Are the arguments aimed at a particular audience?

TRUTH TOLD

In some countries—including Australia, Singapore, and Peru—voting is required for citizens of a certain age.

To investigate more, consider where you stand on this issue. Write to your elected officials voicing your views on whether they should support lowering the voting age.

TRUTH AND RECONCILIATION

Many nations with histories of violent conflict establish truth and reconciliation commissions (TRCs) to help populations heal from social and political trauma. The commissions take many forms and serve many purposes, often drawing support from a country's government and from organizations such as the UN. TRCs are designed to publicly recognize victims, allowing their voices to be restored as they speak their truths on the record.

To investigate more, consider that learning how to manage and resolve conflict is a life skill that all global citizens need. Constructive conversations that happen before things get tense lead to better outcomes for all groups involved. Is there an issue that causes conflict or tension at your school or in your community? Research the issue and develop a peer mediation program that serves as a bridge between groups that are in conflict. Talk with other students, teachers, counselors, and administrators for help. How does it work? Does it help?

- **Research the TRC from one of the countries listed.** When and why was this TRC organized? Was it organized by the government or by an intergovernmental organization (IGO), which involves two or more countries working together? What form did the TRC take (a trial, a collection of public testimonies)? Did it lead to a trial?

  - Argentina
  - Canada
  - Chile
  - Ecuador
  - Kenya
  - Liberia
  - Morocco
  - Philippines
  - Rwanda
  - Sierra Leone
  - South Africa
  - South Korea

- **After learning what happened in this country's past, research what's happening in the present.** Did the TRC achieve its aims? Is the country politically stable? What is being done to continue to build trust between diverse groups?

- **Next, think about your own country.** In the United States, a small number of local communities have used TRCs to confront histories of racial violence. Research the Clinton Administration's "One America" initiative and the Greensboro TRC of 1999. If more widely adopted, do you think this approach could help America confront the truth of its history of racial oppression and move toward reconciliation?

Chapter 3 ▶

Promoting Economic Justice

WHILE MOST PEOPLE IN YOUR TOWN ARE DOING FINE, THERE ARE LIKELY FAMILIES AND INDIVIDUALS WHO ARE STRUGGLING.

How can we create a world where all people have equal economic opportunities?

Poverty is most often a result of lack of opportunities, not a lack of willingness to work. By increasing opportunities for all people around the world in positive, sustainable ways, we can help make global poverty a thing of the past.

● ● ● ● ● ● ● ●

Do all the people in your town have the chance to make enough money? Do they all have the same opportunities? Does each student at the local high school have the chance to attend an expensive college if that's where they want to go? Are any residents struggling to find housing or food?

Poverty is the condition of lacking enough money to buy basic necessities such as food, health care, and housing. While you might live in a town where most residents are doing just fine, some families and individuals are likely to be struggling.

In many countries around the world, poverty is a daily challenge for a large percentage of the population.

What are the root causes of economic and social inequality? In today's world, how does lack of economic and educational opportunity impact people's lives?

POVERTY TODAY

Here's the good news—extreme global poverty is declining. During the past 30 years, it's estimated that more than a billion people have moved out of extreme poverty. In 1990, 36 percent of the world's residents lived in poverty. By 2015, that number had decreased to 10 percent. Poverty reduction has been a major priority of the UN, World Bank, and other organizations, and significant progress has been made, especially in East and South Asia.

Still, in many parts of the world—especially in conflict zones, areas with weak institutions, and regions prone to natural disasters—rates of extreme poverty haven't changed. In some places in sub-Saharan Africa, poverty levels have even increased. Much work still needs to be done, especially if the SDG target goal of "No Poverty" by 2030 is to be met.

Why is wealth unevenly distributed in the first place? What happened in history that created a world in which some people still cannot meet their basic needs? Let's take a closer look.

A boy bathes in a polluted river under a railroad bridge in the slums of Indonesia.

Credit: Jonathan McIntosh (CC BY 2.0)

AN ECONOMIC HISTORY

Colonialism is one major historical factor that has contributed to today's poverty. Under colonialism, a period spanning from the sixteenth through twentieth centuries, white, European countries competed to conquer and divide the globe.

The Submission of Prince Dipo Negoro to General de Kock, March 28, 1830, which ended the Java War (1825–1830) between the Dutch Empire and the native Javanese rebels.

Credit: Nicolaas Pieneman (1809–1860)

TRUTH TOLD

Historians Susan Gage and Don McNair have described colonialism as "a huge vacuum cleaner, sucking all the wealth and jobs and pride" out of the colonies.

The motivations of these countries were economic and political. They took advantage of new technologies to strike into Africa, Asia, and the Americas in search of natural resources such as gold, tea, and rubber. The goal was to fuel industry and open new trade markets to build powerful, wealthy empires. So, people and resources from one part of the world were exploited for the economic benefit of those living elsewhere.

This was the case with Holland, which relied on its colonies in the Dutch East Indies (today called Indonesia) for one-third of its total budget between 1850 and 1872. This money wasn't invested in the Dutch East Indies, but instead went toward reducing the Dutch national debt and building state railways in Holland.

As this example shows, powers such as Holland took money away from their colonies to fuel development at home. The colonies didn't experience any of this growth. Gaps widened as one continent grew wealthier at the expense of other parts of the world.

Colonizers also drastically changed social life in the colonies. Colonizers demanded that only certain crops be grown for export and then they paid low prices to growers to maximize profit. They heavily taxed businesses and pushed craftspeople out of traditional trades. Colonizers also drew their own boundaries, governed with military control, and promoted the idea of white, European superiority.

People in colonized parts of the world always resisted oppression and colonization. But it wasn't until after World War II that decolonization gained momentum. Independence movements in Africa and Asia took various forms, from nonviolent protest in India to armed uprisings in Vietnam.

> While many former colonies have gained their independence during the past 50 to 60 years, the legacies of colonialism remained even in the newly independent countries.

Today, this can be seen in the over-reliance on one or two crops, which causes soil depletion and biodiversity loss. If there's a drought or other natural disaster, the failure of these crops leads to major human and economic catastrophes, including famine. Additionally, many former colonies never fully developed their own industries. Others find themselves in debt due to borrowing money from international lending institutions.

Poverty is also a critical issue in the world's wealthier nations. In the United States, the childhood poverty rate stands at one in five, with Native American, African American, and Latinx children disproportionately affected due to historical and ongoing inequalities. The poverty rate has increased in suburban areas, where there are often fewer resources for social programs and aid, as residents struggle to afford rising costs-of-living on flat wages.

Activists and human rights advocates argue that regardless of location, extreme poverty is a human rights issue. Governments need to act to ensure that all citizens enjoy the full cultural and political rights to which they are entitled.

THE BELGIAN CONGO

In the nineteenth and twentieth centuries, Europeans used force and violence to control colonial lands and resources. They also ruthlessly exploited the labor of colonized peoples. In central Africa's Congo, Belgian colonizers forced native laborers to collect ivory and rubber. When people refused to work or couldn't produce enough, the owners might punish them by chopping off their hands or even murdering them. The estimated number of deaths from the Belgian occupation of the Congo ranges from 2 to 13 million people.

DISPATCHES FROM BANGLADESH

In 1974, millions of Bangladeshis were experiencing famine and economic crisis. Bank loans were difficult to get, especially for people living in poverty. Economist Muhammad Yunus (1940–) found himself in a small village, wondering what he could do about the problem of poverty.

Yunus recognized that poverty didn't have to do with an unwillingness to work. Instead, it had to do with low wages and few opportunities. Poverty stemmed from an economic system that favored people with money over those without it because it provided the wealthy with opportunities for advancement, such as loans, that the poor didn't have.

So, Yunus took the most immediate and direct action available to him—he gave $27 from his own pocket to a group of 42 craftspeople. The craftspeople couldn't qualify for a bank loan, but they did have skills. What they needed was money to buy supplies and grow their businesses. Yunus gave them the money on the condition that it be repaid. Although he didn't know it at the time, microfinance was born.

Microfinance recipients such as Suva Rani in Bangladesh use loans to purchase needed resources and build businesses.

Credit: Department of Foreign Affairs and Trade (CC BY 2.0)

Microfinance is a system of small loans based on trust that offers opportunities to people living in poverty.

In the 40 years since Muhammad Yunus made his first loan, the microfinance model has spread. In 1983, Yunus launched Grameen Bank with the intention of creating a new banking system "based on mutual trust, accountability, participation, and creativity."

Today, Grameen has more than 9 million members, 97 percent of whom are women. It serves more than 81,000 villages. Sixty-five percent of loan recipients have improved their living conditions and no longer live in extreme poverty.

The bank's successes aren't limited to individuals and they aren't just economic—they have a ripple effect on entire communities. They lead to new educational opportunities for the children of recipients, who can continue in school rather than having to leave to earn income for the family. They also create more chances for women to participate in economic, social, and political life.

But the model has also experienced growing pains. These include aggressive client recruiting and high-interest lending practices that authorities in multiple locations are working to curb.

Microfinance is one way to meet the overlapping goals of eliminating poverty, providing quality education, promoting gender equality, ensuring decent work for all, sparking innovation, and reducing inequality (SDGs 1, 4, 5, 8, 9, 10). What other steps are being taken in today's world to achieve social and economic justice? What roadblocks stand in the way?

More than 780 million people live below the international poverty line, defined as living on less than $1.90 a day.

MOVING CAPITAL

The International Monetary Fund (IMF) and World Bank have shaped—and continue to shape—the global economic landscape. Both were established after World War II to promote free trade, or the free movement of capital across borders. The IMF lessened restrictions on foreign trade to allow more nations to participate in trade. The World Bank extended loans for infrastructure projects unlikely to be funded by private organizations because were unprofitable. The World Bank also gives grants and provides technical assistance. The IMF and World Bank aren't without their critics. Do some research and investigate different perspectives on the pros and cons of both organizations. What do you think? Are these organizations effective?

JUST WHAT IS THE WTO?

The World Trade Organization (WTO) was established in 1995 to regulate international trade. With 164 member states, it sets global trade rules, regulates disputes, and holds the power to impose economic sanctions. It has accelerated the rate and pace of globalization, with positive and negative effects. Advocates hold that free, open trade benefits businesses and spurs the global economy. Critics call the WTO undemocratic, claiming that it places business interests above human interests. Critics also note the negative impact of global trade on local and indigenous communities worldwide.

KEEP IT FAIR

Today's global economy is one in which money, products, labor, and information all flow with unprecedented speed across borders. Economic interdependence touches everything—from the food and clothes we buy to the jobs available in our communities. When trade partners work together, they can decrease the chances of conflict—the European Union is an example of this. Sanctions, a form of economic punishment, can also be used by one state to penalize another for political actions or human rights violations.

How have people's individual economic rights been impacted by globalization, for better and for worse?

Challenges related to fair wages and equal pay for equal work persist around the world. Child labor, forced labor, and human trafficking also remain central issues. Plus, our own consumption habits and practices are tied to the well-being not just of other people on the planet, but also to the health of our shared environment. Let's take a closer look at some of the challenges people face in their struggle for economic equality.

Protesters in Johannesburg, South Africa, in 2014

Labor Issues

On April 24, 2013, more than 1,100 workers died and at least 2,000 were injured when Rana Plaza, a garment factory in Bangladesh, collapsed.

In the days before the collapse, many workers warned of the structure's lack of stability, signaled by loud cracking noises.

Their complaints were ignored, and the underpaid workers were expected to continue sewing and stitching apparel for major brands in unsafe conditions.

Rana Plaza was an example of a sweatshop, a factory in which workers labor in dangerous conditions for low wages. Its collapse, along with other tragic events, have led more clothing manufacturers to reveal where and how their goods are being produced.

A Rana Plaza commemoration in 2015

Child Labor

The UN Convention on the Rights of the Child declared that a child's work should consist of learning and playing. Despite that, an estimated 218 million children between the ages of 5 and 17 work, many of them full-time. According to the UN, more than half of child laborers are exposed to hazardous environments, slavery, and other forms of forced labor, including drug trafficking, prostitution, and involvement in armed conflict. The highest number of child laborers is in Africa, where an estimated one in five children works.

TRUTH TOLD

Apparel accounts for 80 percent of Bangladesh's exports.

WHAT ABOUT CHILDREN'S RIGHTS?

There are 2.2 billion children on earth. Of those, 1 billion live in poverty. How does poverty impact children's lives? First, basic needs and rights guaranteed in the UN Convention on the Rights of the Child—to food, shelter, identity, and education—may go unmet. When these rights aren't satisfied, children become vulnerable to exploitation—they may be forced into labor or marriage against their will. Eliminating poverty reduces opportunities for exploitation and offers one way to protect children's rights.

A child laborer in Afghanistan

Human Trafficking and Labor Rights

Human trafficking is when people are forced to work against their will, usually in terrible conditions. A $32 billion business, human trafficking is the planet's second-largest criminal industry. It occurs on all continents, and approximately half of the victims are children. In the United States, teen runaways, LGBTQ adolescents, and homeless youth are most often the victims.

It's estimated that one in three runaways is approached by a trafficker within 48 hours of leaving home.

Gender and Pay

A world without poverty requires the full economic equality of women of all races and ethnicities. Yet, women continue to be paid less than men around the world. Why do you think this is?

Worldwide, women earn 25 percent less in wages than men. In Poland, women earn 91 cents for every dollar paid to their male peers. It's 81 cents on the dollar in Israel, 80 cents in the United States, and 65 cents in South Korea. The problem is even more extreme for non-white women. In the United States, black women earn 39 percent less than white men, while Latinas earn 47 percent less than white men. This means black women earn 61 cents on the dollar to their white male peers. For Latinas, the rate is 53 cents.

People doing equal work should earn equal pay, regardless of gender and race. Closing this gap requires policy and social changes, particularly in the areas of childcare and parental leave.

Offshoring and Outsourcing

With advances in communication and transportation, offshoring has become common practice. Offshoring—or outsourcing—is the movement of jobs from one location to another. Companies often go offshore for financial reasons, to find people who will work for less money or cheaper equipment. Companies also frequently seek to evade labor standards and human rights laws by establishing businesses across national borders

In the United States and Europe, many people blame the practice for job loss, particularly in manufacturing. They also see offshoring as the cause of high unemployment in towns and cities where manufacturing once flourished. But offshoring shows no signs of slowing down. Can you think of new strategies towns and cities could adopt to make sure residents have decent job opportunities?

Consumption and the Environment

The decisions you make as a consumer have a direct impact on both the economic and social welfare of others and on our environment. Today, our world's economy is mostly linear. This means that goods typically have a single life cycle.

What happens to that straw you use in your soda? Where does a washing machine go when it's broken and can't be repaired? They're not designed for reuse or recycling and instead end up in landfills or polluting waterways with toxic waste.

> Look around your house or school. How many things can you spot that will have to be simply thrown away when they wear out?

CRYPTOCURRENCIES

For many years, internet purchases left a money trail. But then, along came cryptocurrencies such as Bitcoin. These serve as a form of digital cash, allowing people to transfer money without leaving a record. While advocates say cryptocurrencies make it easier to transfer money in a global economy, their traceless nature also opens up the opportunity for criminal activity, including the trafficking of drugs and people.

TRUTH TOLD

An estimated 24.9 million people are victims of human trafficking in today's world.

TRUTH TOLD

Globally, 740 million women work in the informal economy, which ranges from small-scale farming to street vending and offers no legal protections or benefits such as health insurance. These workers are especially vulnerable to poverty during periods of crisis, including the COVID-19 pandemic.

This linear model is neither economically nor environmentally sustainable. The resources used to make those products, from fossil fuels for plastics to metals for cell phones, are not going to last forever.

What's the alternative? A circular economy is one inspired by nature, in which the goods of today become the resources of tomorrow. In this alternate model, packaging materials would be compostable or biodegradable. Machines made of metals, alloys, and polymers would be returned to their manufacturers, disassembled, and turned into new products. Renewable energy would power the production and transport of goods.

What do you think would be different about your own life if the world used this model? What obstacles might prevent the globe from switching to this model?

CORPORATE INTERESTS

Remember colonialism, when European powers sought profit and wealth at the expense of humans and the environment? That tradition continues today. Mega-corporations often pursue natural resources—such as trees, gold, silver, and water—needed to make their products at the expense of human rights. This has been the case throughout the Americas, from Guatemala to Brazil to the United States.

But communities often fight back against forces that threaten local ecosystems, human health, and economic welfare. In Honduras, the Rio Blanco, a waterway with immense social, cultural, and economic significance, was threatened by mining projects begun by the government and investors. Farmland was destroyed in a clear violation of indigenous rights. The government and corporations were proceeding with total disregard for and without the consent of the communities that lived there.

The Council of Popular and Indigenous Organizations of Honduras (COPINH), led by Bertha Cáceres, fought back, leading the investing company and the World Bank to withdraw funds. COPINH's success, however, came at a tragic cost. Cáceres was murdered by men hired by the dam-building company for her activism, which had led to the suspension of the project.

> Global citizens need to support and join communities in prioritizing human rights over corporate interests.

ROBOTS!

The fear of machines stealing jobs from people isn't a new one. In the early 1960s, U.S. President John F. Kennedy (1917–1963) ranked automation as the biggest challenge to the job market. Still, as decades have passed, these fears have not materialized. Yes, some jobs—particularly in agriculture and factories—have disappeared due to automation. But that doesn't mean that humans have run out of work. New technologies create new jobs—today's economy is ripe for job development in the areas of environmental sustainability and renewable energy. This changing landscape requires a digitally savvy workforce with strong communication and collaboration skills capable of thinking creatively and critically.

How can we make manufacturing sustainable? You can learn about some interesting ideas in this video.

 MacArthur rethinking progress

Look for fair trade logos on the products you buy!

INFORMED ACTION

As children around the world demonstrate, there are countless ways to correct economic injustice and address related social, political, and environmental challenges.

At Home

Educate yourself and others in your household about economic justice and poverty. Challenge people who blame poverty on the poor. As Muhammad Yunus and other economists point out, poverty has nothing to do with an unwillingness to work or some type of character flaw. Instead, poverty stems from low wages, lack of opportunity, and larger economic systems that deny people who have little the chance to get ahead.

When you buy things, choose products that don't do damage. These products guarantee workers adequate wages in fair working conditions. Don't hesitate to investigate where your clothes and food come from, how they are produced, and who produces them. Do you have questions about their origins? Email the company. Responsible corporations will share information about their supply chains—the processes and resources involved in the production and distribution of their goods.

At School

Need inspiration for how kids can be changemakers? Check out Philadelphia's Springside Chestnut Hill Academy. Since 2016, the school has offered a fifth-grade course on social entrepreneurship. Students research world regions where poverty is common and investigate its root causes. They model microfinancing within their school, making loans and tracking investments to see how their lending improves lives.

To finance their loans, students fundraise at book fairs and back-to-school nights, selling everything from homemade slime to headbands. These fifth-graders learn and work together to make a difference in the world.

You can also promote global economic justice within your learning community by investigating the origins of products and services used within the school. Where were your basketball teams' uniforms made? Who made them? Were these goods produced in a fair, humane, and earth-friendly way? Where did the food served in your cafeteria come from and how was it processed? What energy sources does your school use to power the lights or heat the building?

Use this information to encourage school leaders to vote with their dollars for a planet that is more economically and environmentally healthy.

How can we make manufacturing sustainable? You can learn about some interesting ideas in this video.

social entrepreneurship small loan

Locally

Poverty, hunger, and inequality touch nearly every community on the planet. In many growing cities, affordable housing is limited, forcing people to live on the streets. On any given night in the United States, more than 500,000 people experience homelessness. Food insecurity, or lack of consistent access to food, is another major issue—one in eight people in the United States is food insecure.

You are an agent who can create a more sustainable world without poverty. Use your power!

● ● ● ● ● ● ● ● ●

Research organizations in your area that help people meet their basic needs and break the cycles of poverty and homelessness. Contact them to find out how you and your classmates can assist.

You can also strengthen your local economy by buying locally made goods from small businesses. This keeps tax dollars in your community. Some of this tax money gets reinvested in your schools, parks, and libraries, which makes for a healthy place to live. Does your town have an annual craft fair? Check out some of the cool stuff your neighbors are making!

Nationally and Globally

National and world leaders—of countries, corporations, intergovernmental organizations—need to hear your voice on issues of economic justice. Push for change by petitioning officials. Want to see the world move toward a circular economy? Boycott companies with wasteful practices that rely on nonrenewable resources. Organize protests, make podcasts, and produce videos to pressure decision makers.

PROFILES IN GLOBAL CITIZENSHIP

Florisa Magambi
Location: Lilongwe, Malawi
Job Title: Director, Kibébé

Florisa Magambi serves as director of Kibébé, a social business that provides jobs for residents of Malawi's Dzaleka Refugee Camp. Dzaleka is home to more than 40,000 refugees

Credit: courtesy of Florisa Magambi

displaced by conflicts in various African nations, including the Democratic Republic of Congo (DRC), Burundi, Rwanda, Ethiopia, and Somalia.

Employment opportunities within and outside the camp are limited. Most camp residents rely on food aid and other assistance for survival.

A refugee camp in Malawi
Credit: Bjørn Heidenstrøm (CC BY 2.0)

Kibébé allows refugee artisans to sell the unique, handcrafted, fair trade items that they create. In the process, they earn money to support their families' basic needs for food, hygiene products, school supplies, and medicine. Some Kibébé artisans also reinvest their income to launch other businesses and send their children to school.

Magambi spoke about Kibébé's origins and impact. She also shared her reflections on how microfinance, fair trade, and social enterprise can reduce poverty and promote health, education, and gender equity (SDGs 1-6, 8-10, 12).

How did she become involved in this work?

Kibébé grew out of Magambi's personal experiences. Her first child, Mwiza, was born with a rare brain malformation and died at 20 months. When Mwiza was an infant, Magambi and her husband wanted to do everything possible to encourage her development through sensory play. However, few toys and resources were available in Malawi to support their efforts.

Magambi explains, "So I thought, 'These things can be made, I just need a squeaker and crinkly material, and there are plenty of beautiful fabrics here.'" She launched Kibébé to meet this need. She elaborates, "It was Mwiza's life, although brief, that opened my eyes to the potential of making things for children of all ability levels. We say that she is actually the founder of Kibébé."

VOCAB LAB

Write down what you think each word means. What root words can you find to help you? What does the context of the word tell you?

biodegradable, **boycott**, **circular economy**, **colonialism**, **exploit**, **human trafficking**, **infrastructure**, and **microfinance**

Compare your definitions with those of your friends or classmates. Did you all come up with the same meanings? Turn to the text and glossary if you need help.

In early 2020, Kibébé quickly pivoted to respond to the COVID-19 pandemic. By April, Kibébé's artisans were making 1,000 face masks per day, meeting a critical need for protective coverings in Malawi and beyond.

KEY QUESTIONS

- What role did colonialism play in shaping global inequality? How and where are its effects seen today?

- How could the movement toward a circular economy support intersecting environmental, economic, and social justice goals? Can you think of other options?

- How can achieving certain SDGs, including "Zero Hunger," "Quality Education," and "Gender Equality," pave the way toward "No Poverty?"

How many artisans are involved and what types of products do they make?

"There are about 40 artisans, but they do not currently all work full-time, because we only produce enough for the demand," Magambi notes. "We are trying to grow demand by opening an online shop, because only a small number of people in Malawi can afford nonessential products like the decor, accessories, and children's products that we make and sell."

The Kibébé website notes, "Behind every handmade product, there are stories and inspirations." Kibébé's success is reflected in the stories of its artisans, many of whom are women who have fled political violence.

Magambi shares the story of a woman named Moza. She lost her husband to conflict in the DRC. She and her children were captured by soldiers from a rival group and sold into slavery. They escaped, arriving at Dzaleka after two years in Tanzania. On arrival at the camp, Moza was forced to make difficult decisions in order to survive. She found an alternate path through learning how to sew, and later partnered with Kibébé. This allowed Moza, her new husband, and children to meet basic needs. "We were able to get a mattress, a bed, a table, and even electricity for our house because of work from Kibébé!" she explains. "I live because of Kibébé."

In many of our investigations into global citizenship, we've mentioned how our actions affect the environment. This is a very important part of working on the UN SDGs. A healthy planet is a very high priority! In the next chapter, we'll take a look at how we can work together to prevent and address climate change.

PHOTOGRAPHY & SOCIAL JUSTICE

In the early 1900s, photography was a new invention. Social reform photographers such as Jacob Riis (1849–1914) and Lewis Hine (1874–1940) used their cameras to document labor and living conditions of the poor.

- **Research Riis's or Hine's work at the library or online.**

  - When and where did they work?

  - Who and what did they document?

  - What were they trying to accomplish with their photographs?

  - Who do you think the audience was for these photos?

  - Were these photos an effective tool in arguing for social and economic reform?

- **Visit the U.S. Library of Congress' National Child Labor Committee Collection of photos by Lewis Hine.** Choose a photo and list all the items that you see in it. Who is the subject? What is in the background?

 LOC child labor Hines

- **Re-examine the photo with the following questions in mind.**

  - What is the most important thing in the picture?

  - What does the background tell you?

  - What emotions are the subjects showing?

  - Does the pose, posture, or clothing of the person give you more information to interpret the photo?

  - What would you ask the photographer?

To investigate more, think about global issues in your community that you'd like to explore through images. What's the story that you'd like to tell? Take your smartphone or camera and document them. Come up with an artist statement to explain why you addressed this issue and why it's worthy of attention. Show your classmates your work to invite conversations about your images and text.

Inquire & Investigate

TEXT TO WORLD

Do you see poverty where you live? How does it affect your own life?

To investigate more, take one of these items in your closet and imagine its journey. Let this garment speak through a poem or short story. How many hands crafted it? How many miles did it travel? How did it arrive in your wardrobe?

LABEL CONSCIOUS

Buying stuff in a way that benefits the planet and humanity is an important step in being a global citizen. Take a dive into your own closet to see where you might make a difference! This project was inspired by an activity in a "Rethinking Schools" publication written by Bill Bigelow.

- **Open your closet and remove 10 articles of clothing.** List the item (T-shirt or jeans), the brand (such as H&M or Gap), and the country of origin (made in bangladesh). Pinpoint these production sites on a map. Are most of them on a particular continent?

- **Use the CIA World Fact Book to answer the following questions.**

CIA World Fact Book

  - Are these factories located in former colonies?

  - What is the average education and income level of people living in this country?

  - What are the primary industries and what percentage of people live in poverty?

  - What is the average life expectancy?

- **What country was the leading producer of your clothes?** Research its labor practices. Is child labor an issue? How safe are working conditions? Have workers' rights violations been reported?

- **Take a close look at the most popular companies represented in your wardrobe.** Have they taken transparency pledges about where and how their clothes are made?

Chapter 4 ▶
Protecting the Global Environment

GLOBAL CITIZENS MUST DEMAND THAT OUR RIGHTS TO CLEAN AIR, LAND, AND WATER ARE PROTECTED, WHICH MEANS PROTECTING THE EARTH.

What responsibilities do global citizens have for protecting the health of our planet?

Earth is our home, and we need to treat it in a way that keeps it healthy. This means eating, traveling, and buying responsibly.

● ● ● ● ● ● ● ●

On March 15, 2019, approximately 1.4 million children in more than 2,000 cities across 123 countries went on strike. Their message and demands—delivered in speeches, written on protest signs, and scrolled across their bodies—expressed a deep sense of urgency and concern for the health of our planet.

Young Australians issued the plea, "Listen to our warning, stop global warming." Scottish youth called out, "Stop denying the earth is dying." And across the world, from Tokyo, Japan, to Lisbon, Portugal, to Seoul, Korea, kids chanted, "There's no Planet B."

In an editorial written for *The Guardian* newspaper, Swedish activist and strike leader Greta Thunberg explained why students around the world organized. "This movement had to happen, we didn't have a choice. We knew there was a climate crisis . . . . We knew because everything we read and watched screamed out to us that something was very wrong."

The climate strikers have strong science behind them. Ninety-seven percent of scientists believe that climate change is real and that it's driven by human activity. There's a lot of evidence. Global temperatures are rising—the four warmest Januaries on record have all happened since 2016—as are sea levels. Oceans are warming and becoming more acidic. Ice sheets are shrinking, glaciers are retreating. Snow cover and sea ice are decreasing and extreme weather events are increasingly frequent and more powerful.

> A 2019 UN report concluded that more than 1 million species are at risk of extinction within the next few years.

Seven of the 17 UN SDGs directly deal with environmental issues, while the remaining 10 are linked to climate change through issues such as hunger, poverty, and inequality. These are concrete, global challenges that require action. Everyone on the planet is affected by climate change. Global citizens have an obligation to demand that the rights of all people to clean air, land, and water are respected and protected.

We've known about climate change for decades. Why haven't we fixed it sooner? For many, it's hard to comprehend the impact of something invisible such as carbon emissions in the atmosphere. This allows us to distance ourselves from this critical problem. And some people who do think about climate change often feel overwhelmed.

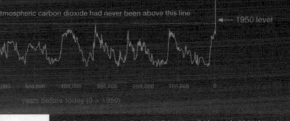

For millennia, atmospheric carbon dioxide had never been above this line

current level

1950 level

Credit: Luthi, D., et al., 2008; Etheridge, D.M., et al. 2010; Vostok ice core data/J.R. Petit et al.; NOAA Mauna Loa CO2 record

TRUTH TOLD

Some scientists estimate that the human population has only 10 years to act in order to avoid the most severe effects of climate change.

It's easy to experience helplessness and question what we can actually do to correct this massive challenge. This might lead some people to deny—and others to tune out—the problem.

GREENHOUSE GASES AND A WARMING PLANET

For the past 200 years, humans have extracted fossil fuels—coal, oil, and natural gas—from the earth and used them to drive industrial growth. In that period, fossil fuels have been essential to mass-manufacturing products that range from food to the refrigerators that store it and the ovens in which it is cooked. Fossil fuels power planes, trains, and cars. They generate electricity for houses, schools, and businesses. But when we process and use fossil fuels, we also spew carbon dioxide (CO_2) and methane into the atmosphere.

CO_2 and methane are heat-trapping gases, also called greenhouse gases. When there is too much greenhouse gas in the atmosphere, heat from the sun gets trapped. Have you ever gotten into a car that's been sitting in the sun? It's hot! The glass traps the heat inside. That's what is happening to the planet. Measurements of the atmosphere show that today's CO_2 levels are the highest they've been in 400,000 years.

In the past half century, the pace of greenhouse gas emissions has increased. This increase has major effects on human, animal, plant, and marine life. Let's take a look why.

HUMAN CHOICES & THE ENVIRONMENT

Every problem is easier to tackle if you break it down into smaller parts. Let's do that for climate change. Here are several things that contribute to our warming planet.

Pollution

Air pollution contributes to climate change in the form of greenhouse gases. Beyond that, pollution also destroys land and marine ecosystems. Whether in the form of pesticides or improperly disposed chemicals, pollutants seep into water and soil, contaminating the fish that we eat and the land on which we grow food and raise animals. This contamination directly impacts human health—pollution stands as the leading global cause of death, with a particularly heavy toll on middle- and low-income countries.

In children, the health effects of pollution can appear as asthma, cancer, brain disorders, and birth defects. In adults, its impacts take the form of heart disease, stroke, chronic obstructive pulmonary disease, and cancer. Each year, pollution kills three times more people than HIV/AIDS, malaria, and tuberculosis combined, and 15 times more people than war and all other forms of violence.

The good news is that pollution is preventable.

The first Earth Day demonstrations occurred on April 22, 1970. Watch footage from the 1970 event. How are environmental concerns different now?

 PBS kids Earth Day 1970

REFORESTATION IN BRAZIL

In 1998, Lélia Deluiz Wanick Salgado and Sebastião Salgado set out to reforest an environmentally devastated area of land in Brazil's Minas Gerais state. For the past 20 years, their organization, Instituto Terra, has tirelessly worked to restore massive stretches of the region's subtropical rainforest, planting and raising more than 4 million seedlings. The results prove that ecosystems can be restored. Today, what was a deforested cattle ranch is fertile woodland teeming with vegetation and home to animal species once at risk of extinction.

Curbing pollution is a key priority of the SDGs. Just 100 companies are responsible for 71 percent of global CO_2 emissions. You can take specific steps—and encourage governments and corporations to take these steps—to reduce the toll of pollution.

Deforestation

Forests cover 30 percent of Earth's surface. These vital ecosystems support 80 percent of plant and animal life and are key to regulating climate. Trees actually absorb the CO_2 from the air as they grow and release oxygen. When trees are cut down and processed for human use, such as burning, building, or making into fuel, the CO_2 that the trees captured throughout their lifetimes gets released into the atmosphere. Fewer forests and fewer trees means more circulating greenhouse gases. This increases the speed and severity of global warming.

Today, forestry and agriculture are responsible for 24 percent of greenhouse gas emissions.

If deforestation continues at its current pace, the world's rainforests could disappear within 100 years.

Deforestation in Panama
Credit: Dirk van der Made (CC BY 2.0)

Rising Sea Levels, Shrinking Ice Sheets

Warming temperatures cause glaciers to melt and ice sheets to shrink. The impact of this isn't limited to arctic regions—it's far-reaching and will reshape global geography. The world's natural wonders, including Australia's Great Barrier Reef, are under threat. Small island nations such as the Federated States of Micronesia in the western Pacific face sea-level rises ranging between 3 and 6½ feet during the next 90 years. Coastal erosion has already swept away key features of the landscape, and food and water security are very real issues. As these islands shrink and even disappear, the people there face exile due to climate change.

The impact of rising sea levels won't be limited to people living on small Pacific islands. It's estimated that by 2100, as many as 650 million people will be displaced by submerged land or chronic flooding. In the United States, New Orleans, Louisiana, and Miami, Florida, could be underwater. Other major urban centers, such as Boston, Massachusetts, New York City, and Charleston, South Carolina, are at risk for major, regular flood events.

The Italian city of Venice is at high risk for flooding because of its location and its weak foundation. Flooding here has worsened during the last 20 years.

CONSUMPTION

The consumer habits of the world's wealthiest people are a key driver of climate change. The British nonprofit Oxfam found that the richest 10 percent of people on the planet produce nearly half of "lifestyle consumption emissions." In contrast, the poorest 50 percent (3.5 billion people) produce just one-tenth of lifestyle emissions. When extreme climate events such as forest fires, monsoons, and droughts occur, their effects are felt unevenly. With fewer resources to prepare for and recover from these events, those who've contributed the least to climate change often bear the brunt of their force.

TRUTH TOLD

Swedish doctor and speaker Hans Rosling (1948–2017) suggested that people take "action driven not by fear and urgency, but by data and coolheaded analysis." What does this mean to you? Is it something you already practice in your life?

Extreme Weather

Record high temperatures and scorching droughts. Hurricanes, monsoons, and super typhoons. Winter "bomb cyclones" and polar vortices. Have you heard about these extreme weather events on the news?

> The world's weather is becoming increasingly extreme.

For example, global warming doubled the likelihood of the heat wave that fell on Europe during the summer of 2018. This period of record high temperatures led to deaths of some elderly people, crop loss, a massive algae bloom in the Baltic Sea, loss of electricity, and a halt to nuclear power production.

As extreme weather events become more common, communities will have to become more resilient. The resource-rich countries of Europe and North America are better-equipped to develop strategies to cope with and recover from these events. This raises major questions about the unequal effects of climate change on people in different parts of the world.

Studies also show that, due to rising ocean temperatures, hurricanes have been getting more powerful and more destructive since the 1970s. Researchers studying historical data found that Hurricane Harvey, which hit the Texas Gulf Coast in 2017, flooded the region with 20 percent more rain due to the changing climate. The type of storms that used to occur about once a century are now predicted to happen as regularly as every 16 years.

Full recovery often takes years. Buildings need to be rebuilt, and families might not be able to go home for months. Schools shut down. Businesses can fail because too many resources go toward rebuilding.

Water Scarcity

While climate change brings excess rainfall and flooding to some areas, other parts of the world face severe water shortages due to extended dry periods, less snow cover, and unreliable rainfall. Only 1 percent of the world's water supply is liquid, fresh water. Most of this rests deep underground, in aquifers that have accumulated through millions of years.

Major urban centers across the world—including São Paulo, Brazil; Melbourne, Australia; Jakarta, Indonesia; and London, England—are exhausting their available water supplies. In some cities, such as Cape Town, South Africa, the water supply has come dangerously close to zero.

> Already, water scarcity has led to warfare and violent conflict.

This was the case in the drought-plagued Darfur region of Sudan, where a war labeled by the UN "triggered by climate change" claimed the lives of approximately 400,000 people and displaced 3 million others. Some observers also believe that a 2006 drought was partially responsible for the Syrian civil war. People who are desperate for water are more likely to engage in violence than those who have all their needs met.

Water is essential to life—people cannot live for more than a few days without it. This basic fact was recognized by the UN in 2010, when water was called out as a human right. Conservation, whether in personal use, changes to agricultural and business practices, or infrastructure repair, is key to ensuring the future availability of water to all people worldwide.

Theewaterskloof Dam in South Africa in December 2017. The dam level is extremely low.

Credit: Sentinel Hub (CC BY 2.0)

CAPE TOWN "DAY ZERO"

In spring 2018, Cape Town, South Africa—a city of 4 million—saw months of warning about the worst-case scenario of completely running out of water. Lack of rain and high water consumption meant that taps would soon run dry. Water would be rationed and residents would have to line up at filling stations to obtain it. The clock ticked. The warnings continued. And people listened. They changed the way they behaved. They bought a little more time, and then a bit more, by adjusting how they consumed water. Day Zero arrived . . . and residents had halved their water consumption from four years earlier. Careful water usage, paired with much-needed rainfall, pushed back the crisis. Residents in other cities can learn from Cape Town and avoid the panic. Use the water that you need and no more and urge public officials to repair leaky pipes and aging infrastructure.

INFORMED ACTION

Personal and community-wide changes can keep worst-case scenarios at bay. We have the power to act to build a more sustainable planet. So, let's do it.

Where do we start? The mantra "Reduce, Reuse, Recycle" is useful when thinking about our behaviors and their effects. Take a look at your own consumer habits and their impact on the planet. The average American buys 66 new pieces of clothing a year.

Each American also throws away 81 pounds of clothes and textiles a year, five times more than in 1960. Most of these garments end up in landfills.

Reducing the amount that we consume, mindfully reusing what we buy, and recycling are simple actions that we all can take to enact SDG 12: "Responsible Consumption and Production." Read on to learn about other steps that you can take to protect the planet.

Home

Let's start with simple steps, right at home.

- **Take five-minute showers:** The average American shower lasts eight minutes and uses 20 gallons of water. Cut this by three minutes to conserve water and lower energy costs. The environment—and the people who pay your fuel bill!—will thank you.

- **Drive less:** According to the Center for Climate and Energy Solutions, "Transportation is the largest source of carbon emissions in the United States. Communities with strong public transportation can reduce the nation's carbon emissions by 37 million metric tons yearly."

If it's an option, bike or walk instead of having your parents drive. If you live in a city with public transportation, choose to ride with others instead of riding alone.

- **Eat less meat:** Do you love burgers? The production of meat—especially beef—has a huge impact on the climate! Reducing our appetite for steaks and burgers places less strain on natural resources and puts fewer greenhouse gases in our atmosphere. Switching to a meatless meal a few times a week makes a big difference. Try a plant-based meat substitute and see how you like it!

- **Buy local:** Just as transporting people adds greatly to the climate crisis, transporting food does, too. Food transportation produces an extraordinary amount of CO_2. You and your family can support local food systems and reduce your household carbon footprint by buying locally grown foods when possible.

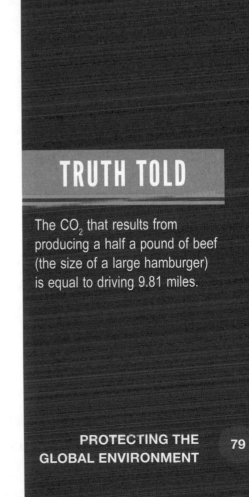

TRUTH TOLD

The CO_2 that results from producing a half a pound of beef (the size of a large hamburger) is equal to driving 9.81 miles.

PROTECTING THE GLOBAL ENVIRONMENT

How do we balance the act of eating locally sourced food with eating food from other regions, which connects us to other global cultures? How do we experience new things while supporting the climate?

● ● ● ● ● ● ● ●

What more can you do to combat plastic pollution? Watch this video for ideas.

 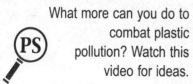

Nat Geo kids plastic

Recycle: In the United States, about 80 percent of items that end up in the trash are recyclable. Recycling saves energy, can reuse non-renewable resources, and keeps nonbiodegradable materials out of landfills and oceans. So, give that soda can and your old math notes new life by putting them in the recycling bin! Remember that you can also recycle clothing by donating it.

Many stores, such as The North Face and Levi's, also offer clothing and textile recycling.

Slay the energy vampires: The electricity that you use—for computers, televisions, lights—is largely powered by fossil fuels. Turn off lights and unplug electronics when not in use to conserve resources. Don't leave your phone charger plugged in when you're not charging your phone!

Reuse water bottles: Around the world, a million plastic water bottles are bought every minute. Most of these bottles aren't recycled. Instead, they end up in landfills or oceans, where they harm wildlife that confuse this trash for food. Do your part by swapping out disposable plastic for a refillable container.

Switch the bulbs: Energy-efficient LED bulbs use 25 to 80 percent less energy than traditional bulbs. They also last far longer than their traditional cousins. The benefits? Lower energy usage translates to less carbon produced, and longer-lasting bulbs equals less waste in landfills.

(Credit: Wonderlane (CC BY 2.0))

- **Bring your own bags:** Bring reusable bags to the grocery store. Plastic bags are made with fossil fuels and frequently end up in the ocean. More than 100,000 marine animals are killed by plastic bags each year. If reusable bags aren't allowed, load your groceries back into the cart after purchasing and fill your bags in your car.

- **Consume responsibly:** Research the environmental practices of the companies that make the products that you consume. Many corporations have committed to 100-percent renewable energy.

POLLINATOR POWER!

Pollinators—bees, butterflies, hummingbirds—are critical to our food supply. Ninety percent of our food supply relies on their work, so a world without pollinators is a world without food . . . and a world without human life. Chemical pesticides threaten pollinators. In recent years, bee colonies have collapsed in record numbers. Many researchers think it's due to popular pesticides, and the evidence is strong enough that the European Union banned three major brands of pesticides. You can support bee health at home and school by discouraging the use of pesticides (hey, dandelions are beautiful!) and by planting gardens that provide food for pollinators.

- **Form a club:** There's strength in numbers. Eco clubs are a great way to build a network of allies, generate ideas, and take action. Clubs can host community clean-ups, start a composting program at a school to reduce food leftovers that end up in the landfill, launch a school or community vegetable garden to reduce the miles that food travels, sponsor guest speakers, and create public service announcements. These activities allow you to educate others and share steps to reduce our impact on the environment.

- **Evaluate school practices:** What is your school doing to be greener? As an individual or as part of a club, you can evaluate school practices and petition leadership for changes. This might mean hosting a community conversation about Meatless Mondays, launching a recycling program, starting a compost program, or discussing alternatives to plastic and Styrofoam.

  In 2016, students in Portland, Oregon, partnered with parents, teachers, and activists to craft a climate justice resolution. Students demanded that climate literacy be included in the curriculum. Their efforts are being used elsewhere to ensure that all young people have access to current, fact-based information about environmental issues.

- **Write an editorial:** Don't keep knowledge about climate action to yourself! Use the power of the word to share what you know, perhaps by writing an editorial in the school newspaper or newsletter or even your local newspaper. Remember to present clear evidence and reasoning to your audience—show them why should they care about the topic and what they can do about it.

Locally

Is your local government acting for a greener future? City councils in Seattle and San Francisco recently banned plastic straws.

Fees on plastic bags in the United Kingdom and elsewhere have reduced their use by 85 percent.

Other cities, such as Detroit, Michigan, are working to build networks of urban gardens and promote food independence. In the process, residents eat more healthfully, beautify their neighborhoods, and reduce food miles—the distance food travels from where it's produced to reach you. Research to see if similar initiatives are happening in your community. Partner with peers and reach out to your city council or local government to promote ideas for change.

Nationally and Globally

Through events such as the Youth Climate Strike and Fridays for the Future, young people are sending the message to their governments that climate action can't wait. Use the library and the internet to track and join global protest efforts. You can also support petitions and legal actions to pressure policymakers to address climate issues.

Activists such as 17-year-old Feliquan Charlemagne, the national creative director for the U.S. branch of Youth Climate Strike, have been working to do just this. When asked why he got involved in the movement, Charlemagne explained, "I cannot imagine, 30 or 40 years from now, just watching the world get worse and worse, and sitting and thinking, 'I had the chance to stand up for change, and I didn't take the opportunity.'"

PLASTIC BEACH CLEANUP

From Kenya to South Korea, policies are being enacted to keep single-use plastics and Styrofoam out of oceans and waterways. San Pedro La Laguna, Guatemala, sits on the shores of Lake Atitlan, a body of water that was drowning in plastic. But in 2016, the mayor and a team of leaders convinced the town's 13,000 residents to go plastic-free. The town government supported the shift with reusable shopping bags and replacements for plastics and Styrofoam. Today, the lake is more beautiful, ecosystems are being restored, tourism is surging, and additional greening efforts are underway.

Youth in Mexico City participate in a Fridays for the Future protest.

The climate strikers succeeded in sparking global dialogue about climate inaction, even drawing the attention of UN Secretary General Antonio Guterres (1949–). In response to their strike on March 15, 2019, Guterres praised their actions and called on their leaders to participate in the UN's Climate Action Summit in September 2019. Another wave of school strikes and walkouts were timed across the world to coincide with the summit.

Other kids have brought the issue straight to the courts. *Juliana v. the United States,* a lawsuit introduced by 21 young people in 2015, alleges that the U.S. government is robbing youth of their constitutional right to live in a "climate system capable of sustaining human life." In 2019, more than 30,000 supporters signed on to urge a trial.

While the courts responded by dismissing the case in January 2020, the youth plaintiffs and their attorneys plan to appeal the decision.

● ● ● ● ● ● ●

Legal actions against corporations that knowingly emit carbon have also been taken place, notably in the Philippines. One case came after Typhoons Haiyan and Mangkhut wreaked havoc on the island nation. The legal action aims to determine whether 47 fossil fuel companies are contributing to climate changes that impact Filipinos' basic human rights to life, water, food, sanitation, housing, and self-determination.

PROFILES IN GLOBAL CITIZENSHIP

Brooke Mayer
Location: Milwaukee, Wisconsin
Job Title: Assistant Professor in Civil, Construction, and Environmental Engineering, Marquette University

Credit: courtesy of Brooke Mayer

Growing up in Wyoming, Brooke Mayer didn't spend a lot of time thinking about water. Whether she was at home or in the great outdoors, water was never in short supply. But as an adult, water issues—particularly those dealing with its quality—are at the heart of her occupation.

> Every aspect of her work deals with the condition and treatment of water and the big picture of sustainable engineering.

Mayer focuses on the removal of pathogens, viruses, and bacteria from drinking water. In this, her work directly addresses SDGs 3 and 6, "Good Health & Well-being" and "Clean Water and Sanitation."

Many actions that you take at home can be extended to your learning community. Organize with peers to draw attention to environmental issues and push for concrete changes in your school and district. Read this article on a whole class dedicated to the climate crisis. Would this be a class you'd like to take?

Yes Portland climate

The United States produces 26 million tons of plastic waste annually, only 9 percent of which gets recycled.

During the COVID-19 pandemic, officials urged frequent handwashing. But what about the two in five people around the globe who lack access to basic handwashing facilities with soap and water? The COVID-19 crisis drives home the need for global water supply solutions as a way to protect all people from illness.

• • • • • • •

She also looks at how to better use materials such as phosphorus and nitrogen, which are harmful when directly consumed by humans, but might be used as energy solutions.

Mayer spent a few minutes explaining her interest in water issues and her views on the importance of creating water solutions for today's world.

What steps did she take to get where she is?

Mayer set off for college with a strong interest in applied math and science. "I started off in industrial engineering, which is more like manufacturing and process design," she explains.

"After my freshman year, I met a fellow student who was an environmental engineer and learned that there's a field where you can apply math and science and do engineering design, but with the environment! So, I switched over and started doing research projects on viruses and pathogens in drinking water, and that was my first real lab experience. I loved it and stayed in the same lab through graduate school."

What's the best part of her job?

Mayer sees the technology she's building through each step of its development, from prototype to field testing. This process, along with the people she works with, are the most satisfying parts of her job. She says, "I'm in the position of being able to do this cool research, through which I get to try to solve these huge, global goals. I get to work with teams of people who are excited about what they do and get great work done. It's fascinating, cutting-edge research, and I get to do it every day!"

What are some of the most pressing global concerns around water issues? How can we address them?

"There are two key issues around water," Mayer explains. "Supply issues, which have to do with shortages and excesses, and quality. On the supply side, we can all be more aware of consumption. We can be mindful of our water footprint, conserve water, and talk about this issue with our families. On the quality side, it's important to be aware of how our actions affect larger systems. Don't litter! This impacts the world's oceans. Decisions we make every day also impact water quality. Are we throwing oil down the drain? Are we washing our hands with soaps that have nonbiodegradable agents? All these things have an impact.

"It's also important to educate yourself about global water safety. Worldwide, there are still millions of deaths and illnesses due to drinking water and sanitary systems. Read up on this problem. Once we learn about it, understand it, and acknowledge it, we can start to apply solutions."

From clean water to cleaning up oceans, taking care of the environment is a critical part of being a global citizen! Another important piece is making sure everyone's cultural values are respected around the world. We'll see why that's so important next.

VOCAB LAB

Write down what you think each word means. What root words can you find to help you? What does the context of the word tell you?

aquifer, carbon footprint, deforestation, extinction, greenhouse gas, pathogen, and **sanitation**

Compare your definitions with those of your friends or classmates. Did you all come up with the same meanings? Turn to the text and glossary if you need help.

KEY QUESTIONS

- **What are some key causes of climate change?**
- **What effects of climate change are observable in today's world? If climate inaction continues, what global impacts are expected?**
- **How can we act to combat climate change?**

TEXT TO WORLD

Can you spot evidence of climate change in your neighborhood? More frequent storms, water shortages, the disappearance of certain animal species? How does this make you feel?

CAPTURING CARBON

Scientists are seeking ways to remove excess carbon from our air, a process called carbon capture. This is critical because global conversion to "green" energy will take decades, if not a century. In the meantime, we need shorter-term fixes.

- **Many ideas for carbon capture are in development, ranging from common sense to the far-fetched.** Research and investigate these ideas for capturing, storing, and converting CO_2.

  - Reforestation (replanting forests) and afforestation (planting forests where there weren't any before)

  - Direct air capture with artificial trees

  - Carbon capture and reuse

  - Ocean fertilization

  - Solar geoengineering

  - Arctic geoengineering

- **Watch a video about solar geoengineering at this website.** Why do you think countries are reluctant to explore this new technology?

geoengineering
Harvard

- **Of the above solutions, which seem like the best options?** Why? What are some other consequences these technologies might bring?

- **Continue your research.** Who owns the technology? Are national governments investing in them? If so, where? Are international organizations and NGOs using them?

To investigate more, record your questions about carbon capture. Research the companies that pioneer these technologies through websites, Twitter, Facebook, and news outlets. Locate key contacts within the organization's research division, and write a letter outlining your questions.

WHAT'S YOUR COUNTRY DOING?

In 2015, world leaders developed a plan for keeping global temperatures from rising more than 2 degrees above pre-industrial levels. Known as the Paris Climate Agreement, 184 countries and the European Union are part of it.

Each country sets its own path for climate action. For example, in the Netherlands, the sale of diesel- and gas-powered cars will be banned by 2030. France plans to do the same by 2040, and has pledged to no longer use coal to generate electricity by 2022. China committed to leveling its CO_2 emissions by 2030, and India plans to generate more than 40 percent of its electricity from non-fossil fuel sources by 2030.

- **Research to find out if your country is a party to the Paris Climate Agreement.** If so, what goals and timelines have been set?

- **Compare your country's plan to those of other nations.** How is it different? What kinds of things are being done at the state and city levels? How is your local community helping with the problem of climate change?

Inquire & Investigate

To investigate more, consider that the U.S. Youth Climate Strike outlines a plan for climate action as part of the Green New Deal. Read the group's platform. How does this proposal compare to your country's plan? Do you think the platform is achievable? Why do you think so many young people are working hard toward climate action?

🔍 youth climate platform

THE BIODIVERSITY CRISIS

In May 2019, the UN released a grim report. This study showed that more than a million species of plants and animals are at risk of extinction within the next few decades. The authors point out that species are being lost at a rate of "tens to hundreds of times higher than the average over the last 10 million years." Studies show that humans are directly responsible for the disappearance of certain species.

- **Research how the following overlapping factors cause the loss of animal and plant life.**

  - Changes in land and sea use (including deforestation)

  - Hunting and poaching

  - Climate change

  - Pollution

  - Invasive species

- **Think about the information that you've gathered.** What role does globalization play in species loss? Why is biodiversity important? What's being done to prevent species loss?

- **Reach out to local conservation organizations to learn more about habitat restoration.** Ask what you can do to promote biodiversity, and share this information with others at home, school, and beyond.

To investigate more, consider that about 42 percent of endangered plants and animals are threatened by invasive species. What invasive species exist in your community? What's being done to prevent their spread and to preserve biodiversity?

Chapter 5 ▶
Preserving Cultural Rights

IT'S IMPORTANT TO CREATE OPPORTUNITIES TO LEARN ABOUT AND EXPLORE DIFFERENT CULTURES.

Why is it important to preserve unique cultures as our world becomes more globalized?

SCHOOLS OFFER GREAT LEARNING EXPERIENCES, WITH CULTURE NIGHTS AND INTERNATIONAL FESTIVALS.

INTERNATIONAL FESTIVAL

AT HOME, EDUCATE FAMILY MEMBERS ABOUT WORLD CULTURES AND TRADITIONS, BRINGING THE OUTSIDE WORLD IN!

THE EXPERIENCES YOU CREATE NEED TO HIGHLIGHT CULTURAL COMPLEXITY AND AVOID STEREOTYPES.

Your culture informs the food you eat, the holidays you celebrate, the language you speak, the values you hold, and so much more. Cultural identity is what makes our world rich and interesting— it's a crucial part of our humanity.

● ● ● ● ● ● ● ●

In simple terms, culture is knowledge shared within a group. It refers to the beliefs, practices, traditions, habits, and customs that people hold in common. Culture gets expressed in many forms—language, religion, food, holidays, music, and the arts are all dimensions of culture that bind people together. How does your family celebrate holidays? What concerts do you and your friends go to? How do you dress? At the lunch table, what kinds of foods are you eating? All of these are part of your culture.

As social beings, we all need a sense of belonging and community. This tie is so critical that the UN's Convention on the Rights of the Child calls out culture as a guaranteed right that must be protected, particularly for minority groups.

Each day, we're surrounded by and take part in multiple cultures. We learn the rules and expectations of these cultures by participating in them. Small units, such as our families, friends, and schools, have unique cultures.

So, too, do larger communities, including ethnic, religious, and language groups, social organizations, and entire nations of people. We all belong to not just one, but many cultures, each with its own particular histories.

It's important to remember that these cultures aren't fixed—instead, they're influenced by individual members of the group and change in response to shifting circumstances. As a global citizen, you can be a part of preserving and protecting cultural rights, as well as changing the norms accepted by cultural groupings.

In spring of 2020, people around the world clapped and cheered in support of the essential workers toiling on the frontlines and putting their own health at risk for the sake of caring for others during the COVID-19 pandemic. Why do you think this became a global phenomenon? What might this say about our human society?

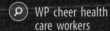 WP cheer health care workers

DISPATCHES FROM DENMARK

Playground swings from Iraq. Benches from Switzerland and Brazil. A tiled fountain from Morocco, neon signs from Russia and China, and manhole covers from Zanzibar, Paris, and Gdańsk. Where are we?

The Nørrebro neighborhood in Copenhagen, Denmark, is a melting pot, with residents hailing from more than 60 different nations. The neighborhood's central, public gathering space is called Superkilen Park, and this space provides a concrete reflection of the area's diversity, featuring elements from countries around the world.

Arts groups, city planners, architects, and local residents worked together to envision this public space, which opened in June 2012.

Credit: Fred Romero (CC BY 2.0)

Superkilen includes a skate park, playground, and green spaces for jogging, cycling, and field sports. It's a place where people from different backgrounds meet, play, and socialize. The design of the space physically demonstrates what happens every day in Nørrebro—cultures from around the world coexist, interact, and contribute to the community.

Superkilen also shows that something unique and beautiful can result from the meeting of cultures.

People don't have to sacrifice their own traditions to integrate into new surroundings. Instead, they can carry their cultures and create something new, something that benefits the entire city. How do we build a world that reflects and respects all cultures? In an age of globalization—in which commercial culture can have a flattening effect on everything from food to fashion—how can we create opportunities for people to celebrate unique experiences and traditions?

How does globalization—the rapid movement of goods, ideas, and people across borders— impact cultures around the world? Is there a global culture of shared beliefs, views, and practices? Is such a culture possible? Let's look at a few perspectives.

A Xhosa bride in Gauteng, South Africa
Credit: South African Tourism (CC BY 2.0)

HYBRIDITY

Think of Copenhagen's Superkilen Park as one vision of global culture. This hybrid space blends and re-mixes elements from many different traditions and parts of the world.

In this example, if Superkilen is the world, its visitors participate as citizens in the global culture of this public space. But, that's not to say they don't maintain connections to other cultural units outside the global culture of Superkilen. These other cultural units could be groupings such as families, villages, states, and countries.

A teenager at Superkilen might be a chess-playing skateboarder of Lithuanian-Jewish ancestry who celebrates Passover and speaks Yiddish at home. Their favorite films might be Bollywood exports and their favorite music might come from Brazil. They may have friends who are Pakistani, French, and Chinese. They belong to cultures big and small, as do their peers.

Cultural hybridity isn't a new process. Across time and space, multiple influences have combined to create new cultures around the world, in ways that are both accidental and on purpose. We can see this in the languages and religious traditions of Latin America, which combine indigenous and European-Christian elements. Accidental hybridity can be seen in the food of Sicily, which contains traces of Italian, Arab, Greek, French, and Spanish traditions.

> The foods used in Italian cooking—tomatoes, corn, zucchini, pasta, eggplant, olives—all come from other places, imported to Italy by way of trans-Atlantic, Mediterranean, and Silk Road trade routes and integrated into food traditions as time passed.

CULTURAL APPROPRIATION

Keffiyehs as an exotic fashion accessory. Cornrows and dreadlocks as edgy hairstyles.

When people talk about cultural appropriation, they're referring to the practice of dominant groups cherry-picking pieces from marginalized cultures and using them in fashion, film, art, and music. When such elements are detached from their original context and reappropriated by a majority cultural group, misrepresentation and stereotype result.

Learn more about the negative effects of cultural appropriation and how it differs from cultural appreciation with this video.

 MTV cultural appropriation

HOMOGENIZATION

Let's take a different view of global culture. Think of a teenager. They and their friends shop at the same stores, listen only to American music, and watch English-language movies and TV. They use Facebook, eat burgers at McDonald's, and drink Starbucks Frappuccinos. These teenagers consume the same fashion, media, and food as some of their peers in Iran, Australia, and Mexico.

With restaurants in 119 countries, McDonald's is a global phenomenon.

Credit: Sry85 (CC BY 3.0)

In the second half of the twentieth century, developments in communications and travel enabled people, goods, and ideas to cross borders with a speed never before seen in history. This wave of technology-driven globalization is not without effect—some observers say that the result is the Americanization of the planet and a loss of cultural diversity.

Critics believe that this isn't a global culture at all, but rather a homogenous culture in which everyone is similar to everyone else. What effect might this have on the world? Some giant corporations benefit, but smaller, more local businesses suffer. In a homogenous culture, we are global consumers rather than global citizens. Global diversity suffers as a result.

CULTURE AS CONFLICT

Some people believe that culture tears people apart instead of bringing them together. From this perspective, the meeting of cultures won't result in Superkilen's fusion. It also won't result in everyone wearing the same clothes and eating the same foods. Instead, it will lead to violent clashes between different groups.

> These clashes will stem from one group believing in its own superiority and wanting power over or separation from another group.

In recent years, white nationalists in the United States and Europe have tried to sow fear of immigrant and minority communities through social media, intimidation, and hate speech. Armed with stereotypes and anger about a changing world, white nationalists violently react to and discriminate against people perceived as different, charging them with hurting national cultures.

This argument hinges on the flawed belief that culture is fixed. It asserts that French, British, German, or American culture is—and has only ever been— influenced by one single group, and that different populations can't peacefully coexist.

This extremist worldview aims to create false, us-versus-them divisions and threatens the promises made in the UDHR and in the Convention on the Rights of the Child. Nationalism is based on the idea that not all people are born equal and that not all people should enjoy the right to equally express their cultures.

WHEN A LANGUAGE DIES

Every two weeks, one of the world's languages disappears. By the end of this century, more than half of the world's 7,000 known languages face extinction, including Wiradjuri, one of 40 of the remaining 250 indigenous languages in Australia with 30 living speakers, and Nawat in El Salvador, with 200 speakers. Languages are threatened by many things—aging populations, technology, war and conflict, migration, and educational systems that promote certain languages over others can all lead people to abandon one language for another. Linguistic diversity matters, because distinct languages contain key pieces of human knowledge built during thousands of years. Language reflects the collective wisdom of groups of people. Efforts to save languages from extinction are underway. *National Geographic*'s "Enduring Voices" initiative seeks to record and maintain languages across the globe. Technology is also helping preserve languages.

🔍 Nat Geo dying language

As a global citizen, you can disrupt this narrative by being aware of white nationalist talking points, by countering their beliefs with evidence and reasoning, and by creating communities in which intolerance isn't tolerated.

Let's take a look at current and past human rights issues that center around culture. Why do some cultures try to control or destroy other cultures? What is the threat?

"Kill the Indian, and save the man." Those words were spoken by U.S. cavalry captain Richard Henry Pratt (1840–1924) in 1892. Pratt was a key figure behind the Carlisle Indian School in Pennsylvania, one of 150 boarding schools in the United States that set out to Americanize Native American children.

The Carlisle Indian School in the 1890s

Before then, the U.S. government forcibly removed Native Americans from ancestral lands as European settlers expanded West. Violence and warfare were key to this strategy. But by the late nineteenth century, a new policy was in effect. This policy set out to assimilate Native American children through re-education and cultural reprogramming. Here's how they did that.

During this period in both the United States and Canada, indigenous people from more than 500 tribal nations were directed to abandon their culture. Children were forcibly taken from their communities and enrolled at government-run boarding schools.

There, they were made to take new names. They could no longer speak their own language or practice their own religion. Their hair was cut. They were given new clothes. They were told that their culture was inferior.

> These children were separated from their families for four or more years and suffered harsh punishments for speaking their language and practicing their culture. Can you imagine what this must have been like for those children?

This type of cultural reprogramming wasn't limited to the United States and Canada. In the 1890s, the American and Canadian efforts inspired Sultan Abdulhamid II (1842–1918), leader of the Ottoman Empire, to bring cultural reprogramming efforts to Turkey. Abdulhamid established the state-sponsored Aşiret School for Tribes as a way to assimilate boys from the leading families of the empire's ethnic minority Arab and Kurdish clans.

SOCIAL MEDIA AND CENSORSHIP

In recent years, some college students have protested controversial speakers on campus, including Milo Yiannopoulos, whose inflammatory comments have gotten him banned from Twitter and Facebook for harassment. But hate speech is protected by the U.S. Constitution, so long as the words do not directly incite violence. This is because, as Henry E. Brady, dean of Berkeley's School of Public Policy explains, "One person's hate speech might be another person's valid criticism of somebody else . . . it's very hard to make the distinction."

The United States is unique in this regard among established democracies. In France, "public insults" based on religion, race, ethnicity, or nationality are punishable by law. In Germany, Austria, Hungary, and Poland, laws against hate-speech were put on the books in the aftermath of the Holocaust. Similar legislation has also been implemented in Canada and Mexico.

What constitutes free speech in the United States? Learn more in this discussion between two campus officials at UC-Berkeley.

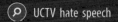 UCTV hate speech

AUSTRALIA'S STOLEN GENERATIONS

Between 1910 and the early 1970s, the Australian government—with support from Christian missionaries—set out to move light-skinned and mixed-race indigenous children into white society. It's estimated that between 10 and 33 percent of Australia's aboriginal children were forcibly removed from their homes during this period. Not only did they lose their families, they also lost their names, language, and culture. In 2007, the Australian government officially apologized to the so-called "Stolen Generations." The government also publicly recognized this policy's impact on victims and their families.

 Broad Abroad stolen generation

Protestors in Washington, DC, stand against the mistreatment of Uighurs in China.

Credit: www.Futureatlas.com (CC BY 2.0)

Similar attempts to strip people of their cultures still happen today. As in the past, these efforts are often led by governments that want to erase minority traditions in order to build strong national identity. This is the case in western China, where Muslim minorities are routinely persecuted by the state.

It is estimated that up to 1 million of the country's 10 million Uighurs have been held in "voluntary education centers." News sources and human rights groups report physical and psychological torture in these centers, where people are forced to reject their Muslim faith and profess loyalty to China's Communist Party. Cultural practices—men's facial hair, religious names for children, and fasting during Ramadan—are banned.

In recent years, hate and terrorist groups that view culture as a threat to their worldview have grown visibly. Depending upon geography and the minority groups within an area, these hate groups target Muslims, Jews, immigrants, women, and LGBTQ populations. In the United States, Australasia, and Europe, anti-Muslim, anti-Jewish, and anti-immigrant violence has spiked.

This violence takes different forms, from physical attacks and vandalism to laws, such as one in Denmark to "enforce Danish values." Denmark and other European nations have also banned outward expressions of culture, including face veils.

Differences in cultural expectations about educating girls lead many young women to put themselves at risk to pursue this basic human right. In Pakistan, it led to the 2012 shooting of Malala Yousafzai (1997–) by the Taliban, an Islamic fundamentalist group known for its brutal human rights record and oppression of women.

Malala's life is now devoted to serving as an advocate for the rights of girls to equal education.

In Nigeria, this tension over educating girls resulted in the 2014 kidnapping of 300 schoolgirls by the terrorist group Boko Haram. Like the Taliban, Boko Haram wants to ban Western-style education for girls and boys alike, which is seen as incompatible with the religious state for which they strive. Education means power, so Boko Haram wants to keep the girls from learning.

Beyond understanding how bias and discrimination can occur, global citizens should stand up against discrimination and injustice. As the Anti-Defamation League notes, "When we fail to challenge bias and bigotry, it can become acceptable or normal. Each time a stereotype goes unchallenged or non-inclusive language becomes part of the conversation without comment, it builds on itself. Bias unchecked can lead to individual acts of prejudice, which in turn can set the stage for discrimination. When discrimination becomes acceptable, bias-motivated violence can follow."

TRUTH TOLD

Five years after the 2014 Boko Haram abduction, more than 100 girls remain missing.

#YoNoSoyTrapacero(a)

Language matters. The words that we use can reinforce stereotypes and diminish other people's humanity. In 2015, 10 Roma children discovered this when they picked up the Royal Spanish Academy dictionary. Each looked up *gitano*, which translates to "gypsy," a derogatory word for Roma. Each was surprised to find their cultural group defined as *trapaceros*, or "swindlers." The kids pushed back against this label with the statement, "I am not a swindler." The swindler stereotype has plagued the Roma for centuries, leading to widespread discrimination. Even today, Roma children in many European countries are forced into separate school programs, and Roma families don't enjoy equal access to health care, housing, and employment, all because of social stigma. Changing the words we use might seem minor, but it's essential to reversing stereotypes. Watch this video to learn more about the story of the 10 Roma children.

 YoNoSoyTrapacero

INFORMED ACTION

Culture, and the belonging that comes with it, is a key part of being human. We all participate in many cultures, and our experiences differ depending upon our larger family and community environments. Teaching others about your cultures encourages understanding and combats bias. But how can you bring people from different backgrounds together in a way that spotlights distinct aspects of culture and at the same time emphasizes our shared humanity?

As a global citizen, you can create opportunities for people, including yourself, to learn about and explore cultures. You can also build settings in which all people see themselves reflected and where new voices are welcomed. Whether at home, school, or in the broader community, the experiences that you create should highlight cultural complexity and avoid stereotypes or simplification.

> Remember that having pride in one's own culture and experience should never be at the expense of others.

Recognize that diverse groups coexist in mutually respectful ways worldwide and this is a goal worth striving for in your own communities. Doing so can be one step toward building "Peace, Justice, and Strong Institutions" (SDG 16), locally and globally.

AT HOME

For most of us, our earliest introduction to culture comes through family. Exploring the concept of culture can start at home, with a walk to the kitchen, a flip through a photo album, or a phone call to a grandparent.

Learning about your family's history, practices, and traditions builds identity, improves intergenerational relationships, and expands your knowledge of the past. It can also help you connect your family's history to the larger story of the cultures to which you belong, while recognizing the unique ways that this culture gets expressed within your household.

> At home, you can also work to educate family members about world cultures and traditions.

Bring the outside world in! This is how you build bridges and help create a more accepting world. Culture is complex and always changing. Don't be afraid to speak that truth to your family and neighbors.

AT SCHOOL

Your classroom offers the opportunity to learn something beyond the core subjects. You're surrounded by diverse peers, all of whom come from different backgrounds and bring different experiences to school. Culture nights and international festivals allow you and your classmates to become teachers. Programs can range from student-led language instruction to dance performances to craft demonstrations.

When planning to share information about your culture, think about your audience. Explaining the what and the why of each practice builds deeper meaning of its history and of the cultural knowledge that rests behind it.

The dinner table is the perfect place to share cultures—and to try new flavors! Maybe you'll find a new favorite.

Within your classroom, you can also advocate for cross-cultural conversation with peers around the world. With Global Read Aloud, more than 4 million readers from 80 countries have connected through literature. Another resource is Generation Global. This videoconferencing platform sparks dialogue between adolescents across borders with a focus on "issues of culture, identity, beliefs, values, and attitudes." These discussions break down bias, stereotypes, and misconceptions between students in multiple corners of the world.

IN THE LARGER COMMUNITY

The arts—whether hula dancing in Hawaii, puppet theater in Indonesia, or Klezmer music in Eastern Europe—are wonderful ways to communicate cultural history, values, beliefs, and stories. As with food, a variety of global influences can be evident in the arts, even in local art forms. One example is son jarocho music and dance from Mexico's Veracruz district, which has Spanish, African, indigenous, and U.S. influences.

How are cultural arts expressed in your area? What cultures are represented? How do cultural arts programs contribute to cross-cultural understanding?

Sometimes, there might be a need to correct cultural stereotypes. Four British teens have done just that with their organization, Legally Black.

Check out Global Read Aloud and make some plans to join the world book club!

 Global Read

A concert featuring son jarocho music
Credit: Secretaría de Cultura Ciudad de México (CC BY 2.0)

This group increases awareness of the absence of non-white people in popular culture and addresses inaccurate and harmful representations.

They use photography, graphic design, and social media to post redesigned posters of well-known movies with black lead actors. They are campaigning for better representation in movies and the media.

PROFILES IN GLOBAL CITIZENSHIP

Jason Rodriguez
Location: Washington, DC
Job Title: Cartoonist/Graphic Novelist, Story Coach with Shout Mouse Press, Biomedical Engineer

Credit: courtesy of Jason Rodriguez

Telling your own story in your own voice is a powerful way to disrupt stereotypes. Through art and story coaching with Shout Mouse Press, an organization that "amplifies unheard voices," Jason Rodriguez is helping young adults illustrate their own lives.

By day, Rodriguez is a biomedical engineer and applied mathematician. But for the past 15 years, he's balanced this with a weekend and evening gig as a cartoonist. Rodriguez took a few minutes to discuss why he tells stories through pictures. He also shared his thoughts on how storytelling breaks down cultural barriers and how books promote discussion of inequality, opportunity, and justice (SDGs 5, 10, 16).

HISTORY THROUGH DANCE

In Hawaii, hula is more than a dance. It's a form of storytelling and a way to connect to the past. With no written language, ancient Hawaiians used hula to transmit history. People enacted poems and stories through movement accompanied by drumming and chanting. Christian missionaries arriving in Hawaii in the 1820s were suspicious of hula, seeing it as a dangerous celebration of physical enjoyment. These missionaries gained an ally in the Hawaiian queen, who banned public hula performances in 1830. Hula remained largely hidden until its revival in 1883 under King Kalakaua (1836–1891), who celebrated its central role to Hawaiian traditions, noting, "Hula is the language of the heart and therefore the heartbeat of the Hawaiian people." Learn more about the importance of hula in this video.

PS

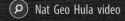

Nat Geo Hula video

"My first book was a graphic novel based on postcards that I collected," Rodriguez remembers. "One postcard was from a World War II soldier to his mother. As I looked at it, I realized that there was a good chance that he never returned. This artifact that he left behind was now in an antique shop for 10 cents, because it was written on and considered 'damaged.' Finding that postcard helped me realize the stories that I wanted to tell: stories of people who are forgotten, in the margins, or who never have their stories told."

While Rodriguez's first project was fiction, his next—a graphic novel collection on colonial lives—was rooted in the historical record. "We went back to primary sources and partnered with a lot of organizations to get it right . . . . We focused on stories of female business owners and slaves and freedmen, not just in broad terms, but on individual terms as well."

How did he get involved with Shout Mouse Press? What's involved in story coaching?

Rodriguez connected with Shout Mouse Press after editing an anthology of artists' responses to police brutality. This project's social justice emphasis allowed him to meet Kathy Crutcher, the founder of Shout Mouse.

"We talked about different ideas for comics, and *Voces Sin Fronteras* was born. This project wasn't just about making books for teens, but about giving them tools to tell their own story in a relatable way for peers and younger kids. We shaped the vision on the idea that it was going to be completely owned by the youth. Even if they didn't want or know how to draw . . . we gave them the skills so that it could really be their project."

VOCAB LAB

Write down what you think each word means. What root words can you find to help you? What does the context of the word tell you?

coexist, empathy, hate speech, homogenization, hybrid, linguistic, nationalist, and **stereotype**.

Compare your definitions with those of your friends or classmates. Did you all come up with the same meanings? Turn to the text and glossary if you need help.

While Rodriguez worked in pictures, another coach worked in words. Every day, this prose coach encouraged the writer to tell a little more of their story, sometimes using prompts. Then, the process shifted to the visual.

How can storytelling lead to a more just world?

From the beginning, the *Voces* authors wanted to address misconceptions and build understanding. Rodriguez witnessed this firsthand, "When these teens talk about their stories in front of other kids, there's a high level of connectivity . . . . Even kids who don't have the same experiences connect; you can see them saying, 'Maybe this isn't my story . . . but I have people immediately related to me who have similar stories.' It really builds empathy and conversation."

START LOCAL

Empathy that's built through conversation, knowledge that leads to action—these are the cornerstones of global citizenship. This book provides a starting point for initiating dialogue, acquiring knowledge, and taking action. So, what should you do next?

Follow the examples of Peyton Klein, Feliquan Charlemagne, the young creatives behind Legally Black, and countless others profiled here. Identify issues that affect your communities and be mindful of the big global challenges that we all face.

In linking the local and the global, you'll become an ambassador who erases divides and builds bridges, paving the way toward a better, more sustainable future for all people and our planet.

TEXT TO WORLD

What are some foods you eat that connect you to your cultural identity? Clothes you wear? Phrases you say?

KEY QUESTIONS

- **Why is culture important? Why is your own culture important to you?**

- **What are three perspectives on how globalization impacts culture?**

- **How can you fight bias and stereotypes and protect cultural rights?**

TO BAN OR NOT TO BAN?

In 2004, France banned public school students from wearing headscarves, large crucifixes, yarmulkes (or kippahs), and other outward expressions of religion. Students could still wear small religious tokens, such as concealed crucifixes. The decision was supposed to reinforced the separation of church and state. Polling showed that 69 percent of the French general public and 39 percent of French Muslims agreed. Similar efforts to ban public employees such as teachers, judges, and police officers from wearing expressions of religious identity have been taken up in Germany and Quebec, Canada. Advocates for the Quebec ban cited the need to maintain a secular society. Opponents charged that the proposal was an anti-immigrant measure largely targeting Muslim and Sikh minorities.

To investigate more, consider that attitudes toward religious expression are influenced by culture, politics, and history, and vary in different parts of the world. Research laws on religious expression in your country, focusing on school settings. Are there limits on what students and teachers can wear? Are there limits on religious speech?

- **Listen to this *Here and Now* interview.** Learn more about the proposed ban on religious symbols for Quebec's public employees.

Here and Now Quebec symbols

- **Outline the who, what, when, where, why, and how of the interview.** What are the claims made by each side? What evidence and reasoning do they use to support it?

- **Looking at your notes, assess the strength of each side's argument.** Consider the arguments in relation to some articles of the UDHR:

  - Article 2: Don't Discriminate
  - Article 18: Freedom of Thought
  - Article 19: Freedom of Expression

- **In your view, does France's law—and Quebec's proposed measure—violate cultural rights?** Why or why not?

ENDANGERED WORLD HERITAGE SITES

The UN's Educational, Scientific, and Cultural Organization, or UNESCO, designates certain historical and geographic landmarks as World Heritage Sites. You can read about World Heritage Sites here.

 UNESCO heritage

* **Explore UNESCO's website to gather the following.**

    * What qualifies a site for World Heritage status?

    * How many sites are there?

    * Of these sites, how many are cultural and how many are natural?

    * What sites exist in your country?

* **Examine the list of endangered sites.**

    * Are they concentrated in particular countries or regions? What current events are happening that put a site at risk?

    * How are these sites being protected? Who is leading protection and preservation efforts?

To investigate more, research an endangered site and use your findings to argue for its preservation. How does this site contribute to our understanding of the human story? What does the world lose if this site disappears? What should be done to preserve it? Communicate your conclusions through a podcast, short video, or blog entry.

GLOSSARY

abolitionist: a person who wants to end slavery.

aboriginal: describes the first people who lived in Australia.

activist: a person who works to bring about social or political change.

advocate: a person who publicly supports a particular cause or policy.

affiliation: a connection to something.

algae bloom: abnormal growth of algae in a body of water.

alloy: a mixture of two or more metals, or of a metal and another element.

ally: a loyal friend who supports a cause.

alt-right: a branch of the extreme right that rejects conventional political conservatism and often voices racist and white supremacist views.

amends: to correct a wrong.

Americanization: the influence of American businesses and culture on foreign people and countries.

ancestry: describes the people from your family or country who lived before you.

anti-Semitic: prejudiced or hostile toward Jewish people.

aquifer: an underground layer of water-filled rock.

artisan: someone who is skilled at a craft.

atrocity: a cruel act of violence.

assimilate: to adapt to the customs and values of a new group or nation.

asylum: protection granted by a country or government to refugees from another country.

atmosphere: the blanket of gases around the earth.

authoritarian: favoring complete obedience to authority instead of individual freedoms.

autocrat: a ruler with absolute power.

automation: a system that uses machines to do work instead of people.

bacteria: microorganisms found in soil, water, plants, and animals that are often beneficial but sometimes harmful.

BCE: put after a date, BCE stands for Before Common Era and counts down to zero. CE stands for Common Era and counts up from zero. This book was printed in 2020 CE.

bias: a tendency to see things a certain way, perhaps unreasonably or unfairly.

bigotry: intolerance for anyone with a different religion, race, or belief system.

biodegradable: something that living organisms can break down.

biodiversity: many different species of plants and animals living in an area.

blockade: a way to prevent people or things from entering or leaving a specific place.

Bollywood: India's Hindi-language film industry, based largely in Mumbai.

border: a line separating two political or geographical areas, especially countries.

boycott: to refuse to buy certain goods or use certain services as a form of protest.

bystander: an onlooker of an incident or event who doesn't take part.

capital: money used to start or expand a business. Also the city where the government of a state or country is based.

carbon emissions: the release of carbon dioxide and other carbon gases into the atmosphere.

carbon footprint: the direct effect an individual's actions and lifestyle have on the environment in terms of carbon dioxide emissions, which contribute to global warming.

charter: a document that spells out the goals and rights of an organization or city.

circular economy: an economic model that favors reuse and rejects single-use products and materials.

citizen: a person who has all the rights and responsibilities that come with being a full member of a country.

citizenship: legally belonging to a country and having the rights and protection of that country.

civic: relating to duty and responsibility to community.

civilian: someone who is not a member of the military or police.

civil liberties: individual rights that are guaranteed by law in democracies. In the United States, these include freedom of religion, freedom of speech, freedom of the press, freedom of assembly, and freedom to petition the government.

civil rights: the basic rights that all citizens of a society are supposed to have, such as the right to vote.

civil rights movement: in America, the struggle by African Americans in the 1950s and 1960s to achieve equality to whites in employment, housing, education, and more.

civil war: a war between citizens of the same country.

climate: average weather patterns in an area during a period of many years.

climate change: a change in long term weather patterns, which can happen through natural or manmade processes. Earth's climate is currently experiencing a climate crisis with record-breaking climate change symptoms, such as rising sea levels and species endangerment.

climate literacy: an understanding of your influence on climate and climate's influence on you and society.

coexist: to live together.

collaborate: to work together with other people.

collective: done by people acting as a group.

colonial: relating to a system or period in which one country rules another.

colonialism: a situation in which one country rules another.

colonization: the action or process of settling among and establishing control over the people of an area.

commercial: relating to the buying and selling of goods or services, with the purpose of making money.

community: a group of people who live in the same place or who share key characteristics such as religion or language.

complementary: combining in a way as to enhance the qualities of each other or another.

compliance: to meet established standards or rules.

compostable: a material that can break down and rot in a compost heap.

conflict resolution: peacefully resolving a disagreement by making sure each side has at least some of its needs met.

conservation: managing and protecting something, such as natural resources or an archaeological site.

constitution: a document containing a country's basic laws and governing principles.

consume: to eat or drink or use up a resource.

contamination: the presence of harmful substances such as pollutants in water, soil, or air.

corruption: the dishonest or illegal behavior of people in power.

cryptocurrency: an untraceable digital form of money.

culture: a group of people who share beliefs and a way of life.

cultural: relating to the behaviors, beliefs, and way of life of a group of people.

cultural reprogramming: an intentional, government-led effort to strip a person or group of their culture and replace it with other beliefs, languages, and practices.

deforestation: the act of completely cutting down and clearing trees.

dehumanize: to take away positive human qualities.

delegate: a person sent to a meeting as a representative of a larger group of people or a specific area of the country.

dignity: being worthy of honor or respect.

diplomat: an official who represents a country in foreign political affairs.

disarmament: to reduce or withdraw military forces and weapons.

discrimination: the unfair treatment of a person or a group of people because of who they are.

disinformation: intentionally false or misleading information intended to deceive a target audience.

displaced: forced from one's home due to war or natural disaster.

disproportionately: to an extent that is too large or too small compared to something else.

dissent: to disagree with a widely held opinion.

dissident: a person who disagrees with a widely held opinion.

diverse: many different people or things.

GLOSSARY

drought: a long period of dry weather, especially one that damages crops.

economics: the material welfare of humankind.

ecosystem: a community of living and nonliving things and their environment. Living things are plants, animals, and insects. Nonliving things are soil, rocks, and water.

emissions: the production and discharge of something, such as exhaust from a car.

empathy: the ability to share the feelings of others.

entrepreneurship: taking a risk to start a new business.

environment: the natural world in which people, animals, and plants live.

epidemic: a disease that hits large groups at the same time and spreads quickly.

epidemiologist: a scientist who specializes in infectious disease.

equality: being treated the same, with the same rights and opportunities as others.

eradication: complete elimination.

erosion: the gradual wearing away of soil by water or wind.

ethnic cleansing: the mass expulsion or killing of an unwanted group.

ethnicity: the cultural identity of a person, including language, religion, nationality, customs, and ancestry.

exile: banished from living in a certain place.

exploit: to use and benefit from something or to benefit unfairly from someone else's work.

extinction: the death of an entire species so that it no longer exists.

extremism: the holding of extreme political or religious views.

fair trade: trade in which fair prices are paid to producers in developing countries.

famine: a period of great hunger and lack of food for a large population.

food insecurity: the threat or experience of not having food.

fossil fuel: a fuel made from the remains of plants and animals that lived millions of years ago. Coal, oil, and natural gas are fossil fuels.

freedom: the ability to choose and act without constraints.

fundamental: basic or central.

fundamentalist: a religious view in which a person rigidly follows fundamental principles.

gender: male or female, and their roles or behavior defined by society.

gender equality: when genders are treated and considered as equals.

gender expression: the way in which a person expresses their gender identity, typically through their appearance, dress, and behavior.

gender identity: a person's internal sense of being male, female, some combination of male and female, or neither male nor female.

gender non-conforming: describes a person whose gender identity does not conform to the prevailing ideas or practices of gender.

genocide: the deliberate killing of a large group of people based on race, ethnicity, or nationality.

geoengineering: the manipulation of earth's processes with technology to try to halt and counteract the effects of global warming.

ghetto: a section of a city inhabited by one minority group.

global: relating to the entire world.

global warming: an increase in the earth's average temperatures, enough to cause climate change.

globalization: the integration of the world economy and populations through trade, money, and labor.

Great Depression: a severe economic downturn during the late 1920s and 1930s that spread around the world.

greenhouse gas: a gas such as water vapor, carbon dioxide, and methane that traps heat and contributes to warming temperatures.

habitat: a plant or animal's home, which supplies it with food, water, and shelter.

hate speech: abusive, threatening speech based in prejudice that targets a specific group.

Holocaust: the murder of at least 6 million Jews and millions of other persecuted groups by Nazi Germany during World War II.

homogenization: to make the same.

homosexual: a person who is sexually attracted to others of the same gender.

human rights: the rights that belong to all people, such as freedom from torture, the right to live, and freedom from slavery.

human trafficking: illegally transporting people from one country to another to force them to work without pay.

humanitarian: having to do with helping the welfare or happiness of people.

hybrid: something that is composed of two different things.

identity: the unique characteristics of a person, country, or group.

immigrant: a person who comes to live in another country.

immigration: moving to a new country to live there.

incarceration: being imprisoned.

indigenous: describes a person who is a native to a place.

inequality: differences in opportunity and treatment based on social, ethnic, racial, or economic qualities.

infectious: able to spread quickly from one person to others.

Informal economy: economic activities or jobs that are not regulated or legally protected by the government.

infrastructure: the basic physical and organizational structures and facilities, such as buildings, roads, and power supplies, needed for the operation of a society or enterprise.

injustice: something that is very unfair or unequal.

innovation: a new invention or way of doing something.

interdependence: to rely on one another, to be connected.

internment camp: a place where people are confined or imprisoned.

interrogation: the process of asking someone a lot of questions in an angry or threatening way in order to get information.

intolerance: the unwillingness to accept views, beliefs, or behavior that differ from one's own.

invasive species: a species that is not native to an ecosystem and that is harmful to the ecosystem in some way.

justice: fair action or treatment based on the law.

LGBTQ: lesbian, gay, bisexual, transgender, queer.

linear economy: an economy in which items and products are designed for single-use.

linguistic: having to do with the study of languages.

literacy: the ability to read and write.

lobby: to try to influence legislators on an issue.

Magna Carta: a British document written in 1215 that guaranteed fundamental rights and liberties. Its principles were used by America's Founding Fathers when they drafted the Declaration of Independence and the U.S. Constitution.

mainstream: the prevailing thoughts, influences, or activities of a society or a group.

metaphor: a way to describe something by saying it is something else.

microfinance: also known as microcredit. A system of making small loans with low-interest rates to businesses and entrepreneurs with little or no credit history.

migrant: someone who moves from place to place, usually to find work.

militia: civilians who band together to act in a military-like fashion.

monarchy: a form of government where all power is given to a single individual, a king or queen.

monsoon: a wind system in Asia that brings heavy rains for one part of the year and almost no rain the rest of the year.

moral: relating to right and wrong behavior and character.

national: relating to the entire country.

national debt: the total amount of money a country owes.

GLOSSARY

nationalism: an extreme form of patriotism, especially marked by a feeling of superiority over other countries.

nationalist: supporting a belief that one's own country is superior to others and placing primary emphasis on the promotion of its culture and interests.

natural disaster: a natural event, such as a fire or flood, that causes great damage.

natural resource: something found in nature that is useful to humans, such as water to drink, trees to burn and build with, and fish to eat.

Nazi: the main political party of Germany before and during World War II.

neo-Nazi: a subgroup of right-wing extremism that follows principles from Nazi doctrine and is typically anti-Semitic.

NGO: a nongovernmental organization that is nonprofit and set up by ordinary people, usually to help people or the environment.

nonbinary: gender identities that are not exclusively masculine or feminine.

nonrenewable: a resource such as coal or oil that, once used, is gone forever.

norm: something that's normal or usual.

nuclear power: power produced by splitting atoms, the tiniest pieces of matter.

occupation: the seizure and control of an area.

offshoring: moving business operations overseas to save costs.

opposition: resistance or dissent, expressed in action or argument.

oppression: a situation where people are governed in an unfair or cruel way.

ordinance: a law created by a town or city.

outsourcing: contracting workers abroad for jobs that have traditionally been performed by a domestic labor force.

pandemic: an epidemic that happens across a large area, on more than one continent.

parable: a short story designed to teach or illustrate religious beliefs or moral lessons.

paradox: a seemingly absurd or wrong statement that actually proves to be true.

pathogen: a bacteria, virus, or other microorganism that can cause disease.

peer: a person in your group.

persecution: hostility and ill-treatment, often because of race, religion, or nationality.

pesticide: a chemical used to kill pests such as insects.

petition: a collection of signatures, signed by a group of people, requesting that a change be made.

poaching: breaking the rules and hunting where and when you're not supposed to.

politics: the business of governments serving citizens.

poll tax: a payment to the government that was sometimes required before a person was allowed the right to vote.

polymer: a large molecule composed of many repeated subunits.

poverty: having little money or few material possessions.

prejudice: an unfair feeling of dislike for a person or group, usually based on gender, race, or religion.

privileged: having rights or benefits that are given to only some people.

propaganda: biased, misleading, or false information that is promoted to persuade people to believe a certain viewpoint.

prostitution: to have sex in exchange for money.

prototype: an early version of a design used for testing.

race: a group of people of common ancestry who share certain physical characteristics, such as skin color.

racial profiling: the use of race or ethnicity as grounds for suspecting someone of having committed a crime.

ration: to limit the amount of something to be used each week or month.

reason: thinking in an orderly, sensible way.

recidivism: to repeat an offense or relapse into crime after serving a sentence.

reconciliation: a situation where people who have argued put aside their differences and become friendly again.

refuge: a place that gives protection.

refugee: a person who has been forced to leave their country for reasons of race, religion, nationality, membership of a particular social group, or political opinion.

regime: the government in power.

repressive: inhibiting or restraining the freedom of a person or group of people.

resilient: able to recover from physical or mental injury.

resources: something a country has that supports its wealth, such as oil, water, food, money, and land.

responsibility: a moral duty to behave in a particular way.

restorative justice: an alternative to traditional forms of justice that focuses on rehabilitating offenders and reconciliation with those harmed by their actions.

rights: what is due to a person naturally or legally.

sanction: a penalty for disobeying a law or rule.

sanitation: conditions relating to public health, especially the provision of clean drinking water and adequate sewage disposal.

scapegoat: someone or something blamed for a failure.

secular: not religious.

segregation: the practice of keeping people of different races, genders, or religions separate from each other.

sexual orientation: a person's sexual identity in relation to the gender to which they are attracted.

social: living in groups.

soil depletion: the loss of key nutrients from the soil due to overfarming and poor land management.

sovereign: having supreme or ultimate power.

Soviet Union: a country that existed from 1922 until 1991. Russia was part of the Soviet Union.

species: a group of living things that are closely related and can produce offspring.

stereotype: an overly simple picture or prejudiced opinion of a person, group, or thing.

stigma: a mark of shame or discredit.

strike: an organized protest by a group of people who refuse to continue their usual routines in order to bring about change in a chosen area.

sub-Saharan Africa: the part of Africa that is south of the Sahara Desert.

suffrage: the right to vote in political elections.

supply chain: the chain of events in producing and distributing a product.

suppress: to prevent something from happening.

sustainable: something that can be maintained at a certain level or rate.

Sustainable Development Goals (SDGs): a set of goals and plans for improving the world, produced by the United Nations in 2015 and meant to be fulfilled by 2030.

sweatshop: a factory or workshop where people work long hours in poor conditions and for low pay.

technology: the tools, methods, and systems used to solve a problem or do work.

trade: buying and selling goods and services.

trauma: a deeply distressing or disturbing experience.

typhoon: the name for a hurricane over the western Pacific Ocean.

unalienable: something that cannot be taken away or denied.

United Nations (UN): an international organization created to promote peace and cooperation among nations

universal: used or understood by everyone.

vaccine hesitancy: reluctance to get vaccines due to fears about negative side effects.

violation: the breaking of a law or agreement.

virus: a non-living, microscopic particle that can cause disease.

visa: a document that allows the holder to enter, leave, or stay for a specific period of time in a country.

vulnerable: exposed to harm.

welfare: the health and happiness of people.

white nationalist: a person who holds militant, white supremacist views.

white supremacist: a person who holds the racist belief that white people are superior to those of all other races.

work ethic: a set of values that promotes hard work.

xenophobia: an intense or irrational dislike or fear of people from other countries.

RESOURCES

BOOKS

Fiction

Al Mansour, Haiffa. *The Green Bicycle*. Puffin, 2016.

Chanani, Nidhi. *Pashmina*. First Second Books, 2017.

Gratz, Alan. *Refugee*. Scholastic, 2017.

Hiranandani, Veera. *The Night Diary*. Puffin, 2019.

Perkins, Mitali. *Tiger Boy*. Charlesbridge, 2017.

Nonfiction and Memoir

Alabed, Bana. *Dear World: A Syrian Girl's Story of War and a Plea for Peace*. Simon & Schuster, 2017.

Braun, Eric. *Taking Action for Civil and Political Rights*. Lerner Publishing, 2017.

Cooke, Tim. *Human Rights*. Cavendish Square, 2018.

Gottlieb, Iris. *Seeing Gender: An Illustrated Guide to Identity and Expression*. Chronicle Books, 2019.

Latin American Youth Center. *Voces Sin Fronteras: Our Stories, Our Truth*. Shout Mouse Press, 2018.

Mooney, Carla. *Globalization: Why We Care About Faraway Events*. Nomad Press, 2018.

Peterson, Bob, and Bill Bigelow, eds. *Rethinking Globalization*. Rethinking Schools, 2002.

Smith, Roger. *Human Rights and Protecting Individuals*. Mason Crest, 2016.

Stewart, Sheila. *Cultural Globalization and Celebrating Diversity*. Mason Crest, 2016.

Tate, Nikki. *Better Together: Creating Community in an Uncertain World*. Orca, 2018.

Yousafzai, Malala. *I Am Malala*. Little Brown, 2014.

FILMS

Gordon, Claire, et al. *Coronavirus, Explained*. Netflix, Vox, 2020. netflix.com/title/81273378.

Guggenheim, Davis, director. *He Named Me Malala*. Twentieth Century Fox Home Entertainment, 2015.

Hogan, Justin, and Michael Nash, directors. *Climate Refugees: The Global Human Impact of Climate Change*. True Light Pictures, 2010.

Young, Rick, et al. "Plastic Wars." *Frontline*, PBS, 2020. pbs.org/wgbh/frontline/film/plastic-wars.

NEWS WEBSITES

When looking at current events, always remember to question the origin (who wrote it), purpose (why it was written and for whom), value (what insights does it provide), and limitations (what's missing) of the source.

New York Times Learning Network
nytimes.com/section/learning

PBS News Hour Extra
hpbs.org/newshour/extra

Smithsonian Tween Tribune
tweentribune.com

Youth Radio Media
yr.media

RESOURCES

ORGANIZATIONS

Amnesty International: amnestyusa.org/about-us/who-we-are/local-groups

Fridays for the Future: fridaysforfuture.org

Global Minds: globalminds.world/chapters

Global Read Aloud: theglobalreadaloud.com

Human Rights Watch: hrw.org

National Model United Nations: nmun.org

Seeds of Peace: seedsofpeace.org

Students Against Violence Everywhere (SAVE): nationalsave.org

United Nations Youth Association (UNYA): un.org/development/desa/youth/what-we-do/what-can-you-do/unya.html

United Network of Young Peacebuilders: unoy.org/en

WE.org: we.org

World Assembly for Youth (WAY): way.org.my

Youth Climate Strike U.S.: youthclimatestrikeus.org

QR CODE GLOSSARY

Page 3: youtube.com/watch?v=IGMW6YWjMxw

Page 6: un.org/un70/en/content/videos/featured/index.html

Page 8: myworld2030.org

Page 8: about.myworld2030.org/results

Page 13: ohchr.org/en/professionalinterest/pages/crc.aspx

Page 14: britishmuseum.org/research/collection_online/collection_object_details.aspx?objectId=327188&partId=1

Page 20: tolerance.org/mix-it-up

Page 25: un.org/sustainabledevelopment/student-resources

Page 31: youtube.com/watch?v=W9HzRn77Lk4

Page 37: youtube.com/watch?v=lmtePwpTd9M

Page 39: youthcourt.net

Page 41: youtube.com/watch?v=u46HzTGVQhg

Page 43: splcenter.org/hate-map

Page 61: youtube.com/watch?v=zCRKvDyyHmI&feature=youtu.be

Page 63: schloanstomakeadifference.org

Page 67: loc.gov/collections/national-child-labor-committee/about-this-collection

Page 68: cia.gov/library/publications/the-world-factbook

Page 73: culturestrike.org/climate-woke

Page 74: vermont.pbslearningmedia.org/resource/arct.socst.ush.earth14earthdays/the-first-earth-day/#.Xkw_VRNKjeQ

Page 80: kids.nationalgeographic.com/explore/nature/kids-vs-plastic

Page 81: there100.org

Page 85: yesmagazine.org/planet/portland-public-schools-first-to-put-global-climate-justice-in-classroom-20170406

Page 88: geoengineering.environment.harvard.edu

Page 89: youthclimatestrikeus.org/platform

Page 93: youtube.com/watch?v=tkXPGLnDaTQ&feature=youtu.be

Page 95: mtv.com/episodes/yfjryb/decoded-7-myths-about-cultural-appropriation-debunked-season-2-ep-207

Page 97: youtube.com/watch?v=KB7kLNwKEVU&feature=youtu.be

Page 99: youtube.com/watch?v=0g7crZDQf1s&feature=youtu.be

Page 100: youtube.com/watch?v=wikX7V3nXDE&feature=youtu.be

Page 102: youtube.com/watch?v=DqBvpWbmdkQ&feature=youtu.be

Page 104: theglobalreadaloud.com

Page 105: youtube.com/watch?v=BLjwluzYtM4&feature=youtu.be

Page 108: wbur.org/hereandnow/2019/04/22/quebec-religious-symbols-ban

Page 109: whc.unesco.org

RESOURCES

SELECTED BIBLIOGRAPHY

Bigelow, Bill, and Bob Peterson (eds). *Rethinking Globalization: Teaching for Justice in an Unjust World.* Rethinking Schools Press, 2002.

Bellamy, Richard. *Citizenship: A Very Short Introduction.* Oxford University Press, 2008.

Blackshaw, Tony, ed. *The New Bauman Reader: Thinking Sociologically in Liquid Modern Times.* Manchester University Press, 2016.

Cabrera, Luis. *The Practice of Global Citizenship.* Cambridge University Press, 2010.

Go, Julian. *Postcolonial Thought and Social Theory.* Oxford University Press, 2016.

Hans, Rosling, et al. *Factfulness: Ten Reasons We're Wrong About the World—and Why Things Are Better Than You Think.* Flatiron Books, 2020.

Harari, Yuval Noah. *21 Lessons for the 21st Century.* Vintage, 2019.

Mansilla, Veronica Boix, and Anthony Jackson. *Educating for Global Competence: Preparing Our Youth to Engage the World.* Asia Society, 2011.

Reimers, Fernando M., et al. *Empowering Global Citizens: A World Course.* CreateSpace Independent Publishing Platform, 2016.

INDEX

INDEX